Knitted Toys

14 Cute Toys to Knit

Tatyana Korobkova

DenizasToysJoys

Tuva Publishing
www.tuvapublishing.com

Address Merkez Mah. Cavusbasi Cad. No:71
Cekmekoy - Istanbul 34782 / Turkey
Tel +9 0216 642 62 62

Knitted Toys

First Print 2016 / April

All Global Copyrights Belongs To
Tuva Tekstil ve Yayıncılık Ltd. Şti.

Content Knitting

Editor in Chief Ayhan DEMİRPEHLİVAN
Project Editor Kader DEMİRPEHLİVAN
Designer Tatyana KOROBKOVA (DenizasToysJoys)
Technical Editors Donna JONES, Leyla ARAS, Büşra ESER
Graphic Designers Ömer ALP, Abdullah BAYRAKÇI
Assistant Zilal ÖNEL
Photograph Tuva Publishing
Illustrator Anna Starostenko (Magic Dolls)

ISBN 978-605-9192-15-6

Printing House
Bilnet Matbaacılık ve Ambalaj San. A.Ş.

Preface

My story with making toys started in a town at the coast of Baikal Lake, the oldest and deepest lake of the world. I learned my first stitch from my mother at 4 years of age.

I took my hand to needle and wool again years later as a result of a serious health problem. It became a kind of therapy for me to knit these beautiful dolls during my illness and helped me to hold on to life. I remembered my childhood and happy memories while knitting. What started as a therapy during that period of my life transformed into designing different dolls and sharing them with my friends and family at the end of the day. As a result of nice comments on my doll designs I decided to share them on my blog and sell their patterns online as well. The knitting adventure that started five years ago in my life, continues now with this book.

This beautiful book contains 14 different doll projects and appeals to knitters of all levels of skills. In each project you will find detailed instructions of one doll with its clothes or accessories. Some dolls even have their own toys as an accessory.

All projects in this book are made with DMC Woolly, Natura and Natura XL yarn using double pointed needles. Besides the general knitting techniques, you will find step-by-step instructions for the different techniques used in the projects of this book, supported with photography and illustrations.

I hope you will knit beautiful dolls and enjoy creating them often.

Tatyana Korobkova

Contents

Materials and Techniques

materials

1. Blush and blush brush
2. Beads, buttons and felted flowers for toy decoration
3. Scissors
4. Glue
5. Safety eyes and noses
6. Crochet hook
7. Wooden beads
8. Tapestry and sewing needles
9. Buttons and half beads for eyes
10. Threads
11. Felt
12. Round nose pliers
13. Needle nose pliers
14. Cotter pins
15. Wooden discs
16. Double pointed needles (15 cm)
17. Pins and stitch markers
18. Toy stuffing
19. Yarns in various sizes

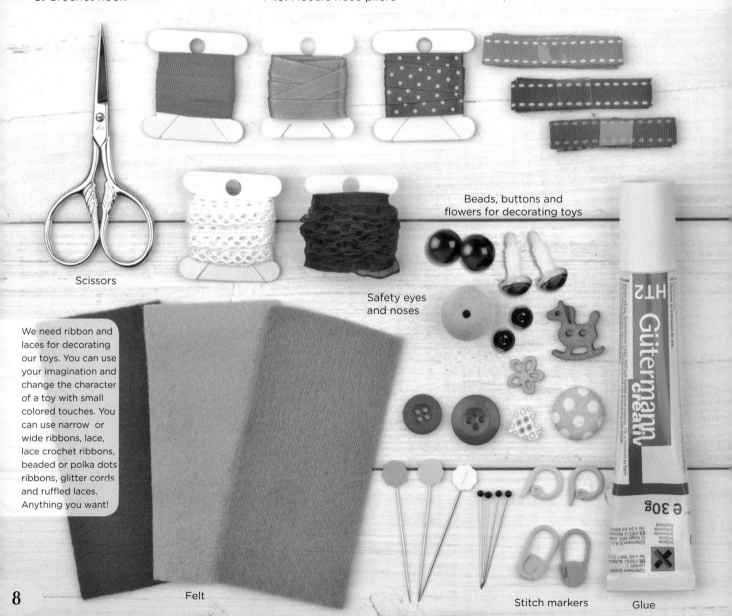

Scissors

Beads, buttons and flowers for decorating toys

Safety eyes and noses

We need ribbon and laces for decorating our toys. You can use your imagination and change the character of a toy with small colored touches. You can use narrow or wide ribbons, lace, lace crochet ribbons, beaded or polka dots ribbons, glitter cords and ruffled laces. Anything you want!

Felt

Stitch markers

Glue

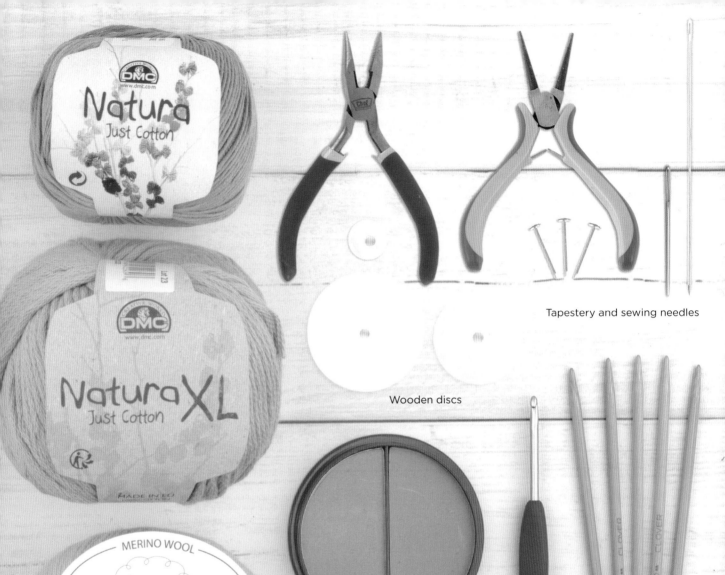

Tapestery and sewing needles

Wooden discs

Blush

Threads

9

holding the needles

Not every knitter holds their needles and yarn in the same way. The yarn can be held in either the right or left hand, the needles can be held from above or below.

Try each of the methods described here and work in a way that is most comfortable for you. They are all bound to feel awkward and slow at first.

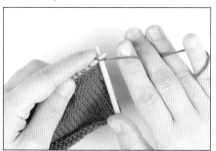  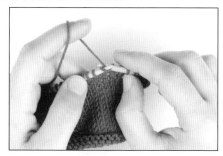

English method (yarn in the right hand)

Left hand: hold the needle with the stitches in your left hand with your thumb lying along the needle, your index finger resting on top near the tip and the remaining fingers curled under the needle to support it. The thumb and the index finger control the stitches and the tip of the needle.

Right hand: pass the yarn over the index finger, under the middle and over the third finger. The yarn lies between the nail and the first joint and the index finger 'throws' the yarn around the right-hand needle when knitting. The yarn should be able to move freely and is tensioned between the middle and third finger. You can wrap the yarn around the little finger if you feel it is too loose and it keeps falling off your fingers. Hold the empty needle in your right hand with your thumb lying along the needle, your index finger near the tip and the remaining fingers curled under the needle to support it (see right hand in Continental method).

Some knitters prefer to hold the end of the right-hand needle under their right arm, anchoring it firmly. Whilst knitting this needle remains still and the right hand is above the needle and moves the yarn around it.

Alternative grip

Left hand: hold the needle in the same way as shown above left.

Right hand: hold the yarn in the fingers the same way as shown above. Hold the needle like a pen, on top of the hand between thumb and index finger. The end of the needle will be above your right arm, in the crook of the elbow. As the fabric grows longer, the thumb will hold the needle behind the knitting.

Continental method (yarn in the left hand)

Left hand: wrap the yarn around your little finger, under the middle two fingers and then over the index finger between the nail and the first joint. The yarn is held taut between the index finger and the needle. Hold the needle with your thumb lying along the needle, your index finger near the tip and remaining fingers curled under the needle to support it. The thumb and index finger control the stitches, yarn and needle tip.

Right hand: hold the empty needle in your right hand with your thumb lying along the needle, index finger resting on top near the tip and remaining fingers curled under the needle to support it. The thumb and index finger control the stitches and the needle tip, which hooks the yarn and draws the loop through.

casting on

To begin knitting, you need to work a foundation row of stitches called casting on. There are several ways to cast on depending on the type of edge that you want. The cast on edge should be firm; too loose and it will look untidy and flare out, too tight and it will break and the stitches unravel. If your casting on is always too tight, use a size larger needle. If it is always too loose, use a size smaller needle. Remember to change back to the correct size needle to begin knitting.

Thumb method

This is the simplest way of casting on and you will need only one needle.

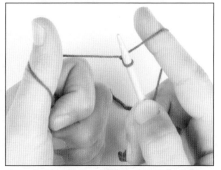

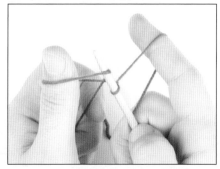

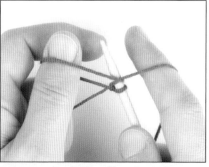

1. Make a slip knot some distance from the end of the yarn (see Knit Perfect) and place it on the needle. Hold the needle in your right hand. Pass the ball end of the yarn over the index finger, under the middle and then over the third finger. Holding the free end of yarn in your left hand, wrap it around your left thumb from front to back.

2. Insert the needle through the thumb loop from front to back.

3. Wrap the ball end over the needle.

The slip knot counts as the first cast on stitch. It is made some distance from the end of the yarn and placed on the needle. Pull the ends of the yarn to tighten it. You now have two ends of yarn coming from the slip knot; the ball end attached to the ball and a shorter free end.

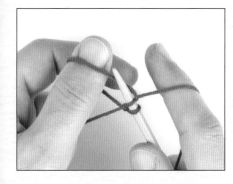

4. Pull a new loop through the thumb loop by passing the thumb loop over the end of the needle. Remove your thumb and tighten the new loop on the needle by pulling the free end. Continue in this way until you have cast on the required number of stitches.

For the thumb method of casting on, you will need approximately 1in (2.5cm) for every stitch you want to cast on. When you have cast on, you should have at least a 6in (15cm) length to sew in.

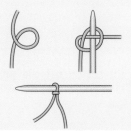

introducing knit stitch

In knitting there are only two stitches to learn - knit stitch (K) and purl stitch (P). They are the foundation of all knitted fabrics. Once you have mastered these two simple stitches, by combining them in different ways you will soon be knitting ribs, textures, cables and many more exciting fabrics.

English Method (yarn in the right hand)
In knit stitch the yarn is held at the back of the work (the side facing away from you) and is made up of four steps.

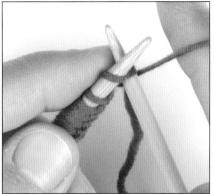 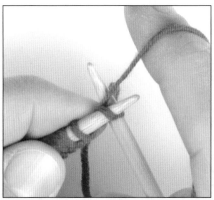 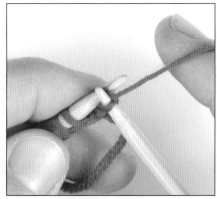

1. Hold the needle with the cast on stitches in your left hand, and insert the right-hand needle into the front of the stitch from left to right.

2. Pass the yarn under and around the right-hand needle.

3. Pull the new loop on the right-hand needle through the stitch on the left-hand needle.

4. Slip the stitch off the left-hand needle. One knit stitch is completed.

To continue...
Repeat these four steps for each stitch on the left-hand needle. All the stitches on the left-hand needle will be transferred to the right-hand needle where the new row is formed. At the end of the row, swap the needle with the stitches into your left hand and the empty needle into your right hand, and work the next row in the same way.

Continental Method (yarn in the left hand)
In this method the right-hand needle moves to catch the yarn; the yarn is held at the back of the work (the side facing away from you) and is released by the index finger of the left hand. This knit stitch is made up of four steps.

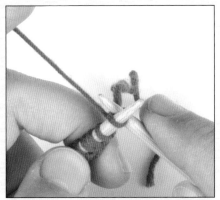

1. Hold the needle with the cast on stitches in your left hand and the yarn over your left index finger. Insert the right-hand needle into the front of the stitch from left to right.

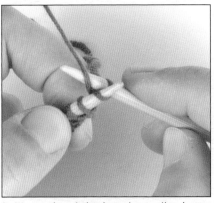

2. Move the right-hand needle down and across the back of the yarn.

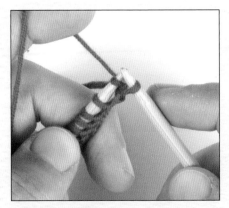

3. Pull the new loop on the right-hand needle through the stitch on the left-hand needle, using the right index finger to hold the new loop if needed.

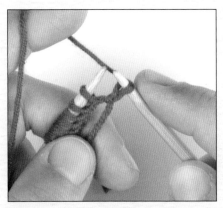

4. Slip the stitch off the left-hand needle. One knit stitch is completed.

GARTER STITCH
Knit every row
When you knit every row the fabric you make is called garter stitch (g st) and has rows of raised ridges on the front and back of the fabric. It looks the same on the back and the front so it is reversible. Garter stitch lies flat, is quite a thick fabric and does not curl at the edges. These qualities make it ideal for borders and collars, as well as for scarves and the main fabric of a garment.

To continue...
Repeat these four steps for each stitch on the left-hand needle. All the stitches on the left-hand needle will be transferred to the right-hand needle where the new row is formed. At the end of the row, swap the needle with the stitches into your left hand and the empty needle into your right hand, and work the next row in the same way.

binding (casting) off

Bind (cast) off stitches when you have finished knitting them. This links stitches together to stop them unravelling and is the simplest method of binding (casting) off.

Bind (cast) off knitwise
This is the easiest method to bind (cast) off on a knit row.

1. Knit two stitches, insert the tip of the left-hand needle into the front of the first stitch on the right-hand needle.

2. Lift this stitch over the second stitch and off the needle.

3. One stitch is left on the right-hand needle.

4. Knit the next stitch and lift the second stitch over this and off the needle. Continue in this way until one stitch remains on the right-hand needle.

To finish...
Cut the yarn (leaving a length long enough to sew in), thread the end through the last stitch and slip it off the needle. Pull the yarn end to tighten the stitch and secure.

Bind (cast) off purlwise
To bind (cast) off on a purl row, simply purl the stitches instead of knitting them.

introducing purl stitch

You may find purl stitch a little harder to learn than knit stitch. But really it is just the reverse of a knit stitch. If you purled every row, you would produce garter stitch (the same as if you knitted every row). It is not often that you will work every row in purl stitch; it is easier and faster to knit every row if you want garter stitch.

English method (yarn in the right hand)
In purl stitch the yarn is held at the front of the work (the side facing you) and is made up of four steps.

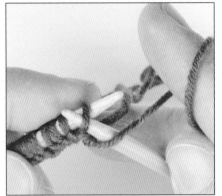

1. Hold the needle with the cast on stitches in your left hand, and insert the right-hand needle into the front of the stitch from right to left.

2. Pass the yarn over and around the right-hand needle.

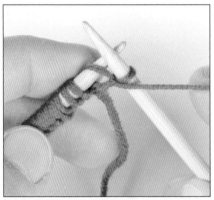

3. Pull the new loop on the right-hand needle through the stitch on the left-hand needle.

4. Slip the stitch off the left-hand needle. One stitch is completed.

To continue...
Repeat these four steps for each stitch on the left-hand needle. All the stitches on the left-hand needle will be transferred to the right-hand needle where the new purl row is formed. At the end of the row, swap the needle with the stitches into your left hand and the empty needle into your right hand, and work the next row in the same way.

introducing purl stitch

As with knit stitch there are two ways of holding the needles and yarn to work purl stitch. The left-hand index finger controls the yarn which is hooked through on to the right-hand needle.

Continental method (yarn in the left hand)
In purl stitch the yarn is held at the front of the work (the side facing you) and is made up of four steps.

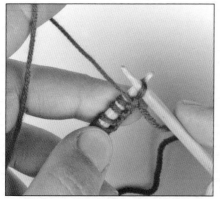

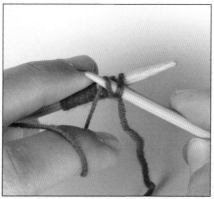

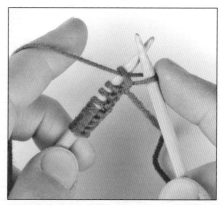

1. Hold the needle with the cast on stitches in your left hand, and insert the right-hand needle into the front of the stitch from right to left, keeping the yarn at the front of the work.

2. Move the right-hand needle from right to left behind the yarn and then from left to right in front of the yarn. Pull your left index finger down in front of the work to keep the yarn taut.

3. Pull the new loop on the right-hand needle through the stitch on the left-hand needle, using the right index finger to hold the new loop if needed.

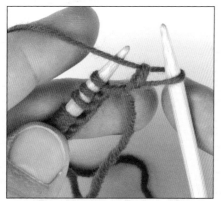

4. Slip the stitch off the left-hand needle. Return the left index finger to its position above the needle. One stitch is completed.

To continue...
Repeat these four steps for each stitch on the left-hand needle. All the stitches on the left-hand needle will be transferred to the right-hand needle where the new purl row is formed. At the end of the row, swap the needle with the stitches into your left hand and the empty needle into your right hand, and work the next row in the same way.

increasing stitches

To shape knitting, stitches are increased or decreased. Increases are used to make a piece of knitting wider by adding more stitches, either on the ends of rows or within the knitting.

Some increases are worked to be invisible whilst others are meant to be seen and are known as decorative increases. You can increase one stitch at a time or two or more.

Increasing one stitch

The easiest way to increase one stitch is to work into the front and back of the same stitch. This produces a small bar across the second (increase) stitch and is very visible. This makes counting the increases easier.

On a knit row knit into the front of the stitch as usual, do not slip the stitch off the left-hand needle but knit into it again through the back of the loop. Then slip the original stitch off the left-hand needle.

On a purl row purl into the front of the stitch as usual, do not slip the stitch off the left-hand needle but purl into it again through the back of the loop. Then slip the original stitch off the left-hand needle.

To make a neater edge when working increases at the beginning and end of rows, work the increase stitches a few stitches from the end. This leaves a continuous stitch up the edge of the fabric that makes sewing up easier. Because the made stitch lies to the left of the original stitch, at the beginning of a knit row you knit one stitch, then make the increase, but at the end of a knit row you work the increase into the third stitch from the end. The increase stitch lies between the second and third stitches at each end.

On a purl row you work in exactly the same way; the bar will be in the correct position two stitches from either end.

make 1

This is another way to increase one stitch and is often used when increasing stitches after a rib. The new stitch is made between two existing stitches using the horizontal thread that lies between the stitches – called the running thread. This is an invisible increase and is harder to see when counting.

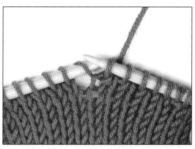

To twist the made stitch to the left
1. Knit to the point where the increase is to be made. Insert the tip of the left-hand needle under the running thread from front to back.

2. Knit this loop through the back to twist it. By twisting it you prevent a hole appearing where the made stitch is.

3. If you are working M1 on a purl row, you purl the loop through the back.

To twist the made stitch to the right
1. Knit to the point where the increase is to be made. Insert the tip of the left-hand needle under the running thread from back to front.

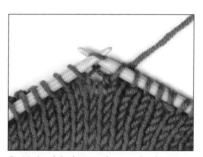

2. Knit this loop through the front to twist it.

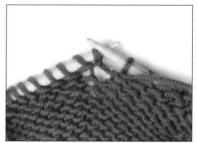

3. If you are working M1 on a purl row, you purl the loop through the front.

Invisible increases

Being able to twist M1 to the right or left is useful when using this increase to shape a sleeve; the increases will be in pairs.

On a knit row, you knit two stitches, then work a M1 twisted to the right, knit to the last two stitches, then work a M1 twisted to the left. On a purl row, purl two stitches and work a M1 twisted to the left, then purl to the last two stitches and work a M1 twisted to the right.

Increasing more than one stitch

To increase two stitches simply knit into the front, back and then the front again of the same stitch. When knitting bobbles, you will sometimes make five, six or seven stitches out of one stitch in this way. For example, to make seven stitches the instructions would read (k into front and back of same st) 3 times, then k into front again.

decreasing stitches

Decreasing is used at the ends of rows or within the knitted fabric to reduce the number of stitches being worked on. This means that you can shape your knitted fabric by making it narrower.

decreasing one stitch

The simplest way to decrease one stitch is to knit or purl two stitches together (k2tog or p2tog). Both of these methods produce the same result on the front (knit side) of the work; the decrease slopes to the right.

K2tog on a k row Knit to where the decrease is to be, insert the right-hand needle (as though to knit) through the next two stitches and knit them together as one stitch.

P2tog on a p row Purl to where the decrease is to be, insert the right-hand needle (as though to purl) through the next two stitches and purl them together as one stitch.

Always read how to work a decrease very carefully. Some of them have similar abbreviations with only a slight difference between them.
In patterns the designer may use different abbreviations to those given here. Always check the detailed explanation of abbreviations.

Slip one, slip one, purl two together through backs of loops (p2tog tbl)

1. Slip two stitches knitwise, one at a time, from the left-hand needle to the right-hand needle (they will be twisted), pass these two stitches back to the left-hand needle in this twisted way.

2. Purl these two stitches together through the back loops.

Decorative decreasing one stitch purlwise

Sometimes decreases are decorative, especially in lace knitting where they form part of the pattern. Then you have to be aware of whether the decrease slants right or left. Each decrease has an opposite and the two of them are called a pair. There is one way to work the decrease that is the pair to p2tog which slopes to the left when seen on the front (knit side) of the work.

decorative decreasing one stitch knitwise

There are two ways to work the decrease that is the pair to k2tog. They both produce the same result and slope to the left.

Slip one, slip one, knit two together (ssk or p2tog tbl)

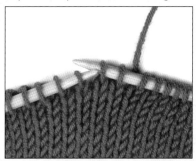 

1. Slip two stitches knitwise one at a time from left-hand needle to right-hand needle.

2. Insert the left-hand needle from left to right through the fronts of these two stitches and knit together as one stitch.

Slip one, knit one, pass slipped stitch over (skpo)

1. Insert the right-hand needle knitwise into the next stitch and slip it on to the right-hand needle without knitting it. Knit the next stitch.

2. With the tip of the left-hand needle, lift the slipped stitch over the knitted stitch and off the needle. This is like binding (casting) off one stitch.

You can use decreases in full fashioning in the same way as increases.

Slope to the right
knit row – k2tog
purl row – p2tog

Slope to the left
knit row – ssk or skpo
purl row – ssp

Decreasing two stitches at once

The two simplest ways are to knit three stitches together (k3tog) or purl three stitches together (p3tog). These are worked the same as k2tog and p2tog, but worked over three stitches instead of two.

The pair to k3tog is slip one, knit two together, pass slipped stitch over (sk2po), which is worked in the same manner as skpo but k2tog instead of k1.

Alternatively, the pair can be worked like ssk but slip three stitches knitwise instead of two.

The pair to p3tog is worked like ssp but over three stitches instead of two.

Central decreasing (Double decreases)

Slip two stitches knitwise, knit one, pass the two slipped stitches over (sl2tog-k1-psso)

Double decreases can also be worked where the two decreased stitches are arranged around a central stitch. Sk2po (see right) is a central decrease. To make a feature of the double decrease with its unbroken chain stitch running up the centre, work the central decrease as follows.

Insert the right-hand needle into the next two stitches as if to knit them together, slip them off together on to the right-hand needle without knitting them. Knit the next stitch. With the tip of the left-hand needle, lift the two slipped stitches together over the knitted stitch and off the needle.

circular knitting on double-pointed needles

Flat knitting is knitted in rows, working back and forth, moving the stitches from one needle to the other. Circular knitting is knitted in rounds, working round and around without turning the work.

working on four needles

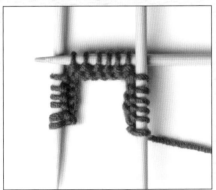

Use a set of four double-pointed needles, adding the stitches at one end and taking them off at the other. Cast the stitches on to one needle and then divide them evenly between three of the needles. For example, if you need to cast on 66 sts, there will be 22 sts on each needle; if you need to cast on 68 sts, there will be 23 sts on two of the needles and 22 on the third. The fourth needle is the working needle.

Arrange the needles into a triangle, making sure the cast on edge faces inwards and is not twisted. Place a marker between the last and first cast on stitches to identify the beginning of the round. Slip this marker on every round. Knit the first stitch, pulling up the yarn firmly so there is no gap between the third and first needle. Knit across the rest of the stitches on the first needle. As this needle is now empty, it becomes the working needle.

> The first round is awkward; the needles not being used dangle and get in the way. When you have worked a few rounds the fabric helps hold the needles in shape and knitting will become easier.

> For maximum control, always use the correct length of needle for what you are knitting; short needles for a small number of stitches such as for gloves, and longer needles for garments.

> To avoid a gap at the beginning of the first round, use the tail end of the yarn and the working yarn together to work the first few stitches. Or cast on one extra stitch at the end of the cast on, slip it on to the first needle and knit it together with the first stitch.

> Avoid gaps at the change over between needles by pulling the yarn up tightly, or work a couple of extra stitches from the next needle on each round. This will vary the position of the change over and avoid a ladder of looser stitches forming.

> Double-pointed needles are also used for knitting circles and squares or seamless garments. Use five needles to knit a square, with the stitches divided between the four sides.

Knit the stitches from the second needle, then use the new working needle to knit the stitches from the third needle. One round has been completed. Continue in this way, working in rounds and creating a tube of fabric. By knitting each round you will produce stockinette (stocking) stitch. To produce garter stitch, you will need to knit one round and then purl one round.

magic rings

You will need yarn, a crochet hook and double pointed needles to match your yarn's weight. The Magic Ring is the perfect technique for starting projects in the round. Since some parts (like body and head) will be joined together we will make two kinds of magic rings. Open magic rings are used when joining parts together, closed ones are used for other parts.

Open Magic Ring

1. Make a loop with the yarn

2. With working yarn on right and tail on left

3. Hold the loop where the yarn crosses over

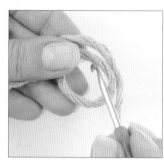

4. Insert hook into the loop from front to back.

5. Wrap yarn round hook

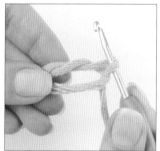

6. Bring the crochet hook under the working yarn and pull up a loop through the circle.

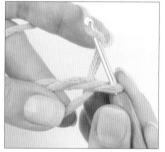

7. Grab another loop and..

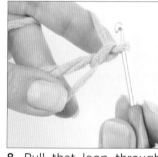

8. Pull that loop through the loop on the hook.

9. Repeat steps 4-6

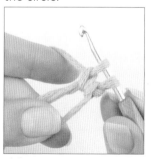

10. And steps 7-8. So that you have 2 loops on the hook.

11. Repeat steps 4-8 until you have the required number of stitches. In general I have used 6 stitches for the projects.

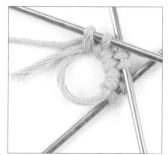

12. Slip the stitches from the crochet hook onto three double-pointed needles.

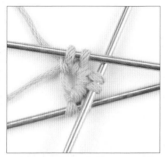

13. Pull the tail of your yarn but leave a small hole. It will make increasing easier on the first round.

Increasing

Kfb= knit in front and back of stitch

14. Insert the right needle into the stitch.

15. Wrap the yarn around the needle and pull through as for a normal knit stitch, elongating the loop slightly. Don't pull the stitch over the left needle yet.

16. Instead, insert the right needle into the back loop of the same stitch.

17. And knit another stitch.

18. Then slip the original stitch off the left hand needle.

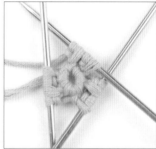

19. Continue increasing into the remaining five stitches.

Closed Magic Ring

20. Insert a stitch marker into the first stitch to mark the beginning of the new round.

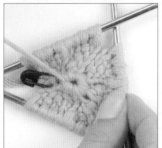

21. Take the tail of the yarn and pull it, closing the cast-on into a tight circle.

22. Pull the tail to the wrong side.

icord

I-cord generally uses somewhere between 3-5 stitches. The I-cord is a tube knitted in the round with two double-pointed needles.

Elizabeth Zimmermann named it the Idiot Cord in honor of her accidental discovery of the simple technique.

1. Cast on 4 stitches onto one of your needles. Note the working yarn is attached to the left stitch.

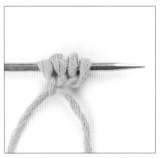

2. Slide the stitches to the right end of the needle

3. With the yarn at the back begin knitting the first row

4. Knit first stitch and

5. Pull the yarn tight

6. Continue knitting across the rest of the row as normal

7. Tug the work from the bottom after each row to help it to take shape and to even out the tension. Don't turn your work

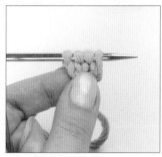

8. Slip the stitches back to the beginning of the needle.

9. Knit the second row.

10. Continue in this manner for as long as you need.

11. Pull down on the cord and the gap at the back will close.

stuffing

The best stuffing for knitted toys is polyester stuffing, particularly if the toy is to be washable. Stuffing is one of the most important steps in the creation of the toys. Stuff firmly as your toy will hold its shape better if you stuff it well. Begin by inserting stuffing with your fingers, taking care to ensure you get into the corners. Continue grabbing small bits of stuffing and packing it in tightly, poking it in further with scissors or another knitting needle. Shape the toy as you stuff to until you achieve the desired shape. And don't forgot that more stuffing is always better then less. Cut yarn and thread through the remaining stitches, adding more stuffing if required, then pull to tighten and secure. Where indicated, leave a small hole for sewing the body to the head.

double knitting

Double Knitting is the perfect technique for knitting dolls. Double knitting always uses an even number of stitches and is worked by knitting and slipping stitches alternately. When slipping stitches this should be done purlwise and with the yarn brought to the front of the work. In the patterns with double knitting you will see abbreviation sl1 wyif (slip 1 with yarn in front).

1. Cast on an even number of stitches

2. Knit the first stitch

3. With the yarn to the front slip the next stitch purlwise

4. Return the yarn to the back ready to knit

5. Knit second stitch

6. Slip the next stitch purl wise with yarn at the front as before

7. Repeat steps 5 and 6 to the end of the row

8. Repeat stitch pattern on each row

9. Continue in this manner for as instructed in the your pattern

10. When you slide the stitches off the needle you can see a double layer of Stockinette Stitch fabric, as if it had been knitted in the round

short rows

Short rows are a very popular way to add shaping smoothly and seamlessly and are perfect for making toys.

In patterns with short rows you will see the abbreviation w&t (wrap and turn).

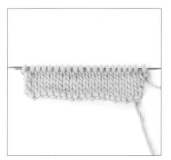

1. Knit as instructed in the pattern until you reach where you will work short rows.

2. Work across a row as instructed until you reach the w&t abbreviation.

3. Bring yarn between the needles to the front of the work.

4. Slip the next stitch purl-wise to the right hand needle and take the yarn between the needles to the back of the work.

5. Return the slipped stitch back across to the left hand needle

6. Turn your knitting and continue working

7. Until you reach the next w&t abbreviation.

8. Slip the next stitch purl-wise to the right hand needle and take the yarn between the needles to the back of the work.

9. Return the slipped stitch back across to the left hand needle

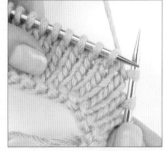

10. Turn your knitting and take yarn between the needles to the back of the work.

11. Knit all stitches to the end of the row.

12. After completing a few short rows the knitting looks smoothly shaped.

weaving in ends

Leave long tails because short tails are difficult to weave in and this can be frustrating. You can always cut a longer tail off after you secure it. Begin working on the wrong side of your work. Insert hook under a purl bump. Bring the crochet hook under the tail. Catch the yarn and pull it under the purl bump. Weave the end at a diagonal, under the purl bumps of each of the row above. Snip off the excess yarn.

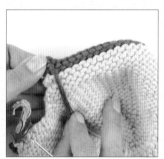

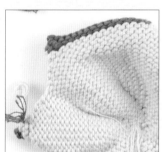

applying blush

For a more "natural" look for my toys I prefer to use my own powder blush. Put the blush on your brush, tapping off any excess and apply it to the toy cheeks.

assembling

Thread jointing
Attaching head to the body

1. Take head and body. If you are planning to make thread jointing then start to knit with an open magic ring. Head and body have small holes

2. Also you need a pair of needle nose pliers and a long needle with a yard of strong thread, doubled and knotted at the end

3. Starting at the bottom of the body, insert the needle in the hole

4. And push all the way through to the opening at the neck

5. You can use needle nose pliers to help with this

6. Continue pushing the needle through the head, coming out on the top

7. Move the needle over one stitch and go back through starting at the head

8. And all the way back through the body and out at the bottom of the body. Repeat this procedure one or two more times

9. Ending with yarn at the base, pull firmly but be careful not to pull too tightly

10. Take the head's yarn tail

11. And pull to draw the centre of the ring tightly closed. Hide the end

12. Do the same with the body's yarn tail

13. Head and body are now attached to each other

14. Now firmly pull the thread with long needle to tighten the joint.

15. Secure thread inside the body.

16. Trim jointing thread.

17. Grab the body's yarn tail and pull to draw the centre of the ring tightly closed. Hide the end.

thread jointing

Attaching arms to the body

The arms are sewn through the body. Mark the position for the arms. Insert the needle at that point. Push the needle through the body and out at the opposite side. Insert needle into the top of one of the arms from the inside to the outside. Taking a small stitch, go all the way back through the arm and the body and out of the other side. Go through the other arm from the inside to the outside. Taking a small stitch, go all the way back though the arm and body and out of the outside of the first arm. Repeat this procedure one or two more times, gently pulling the thread to tighten the joint with each pass, being careful not to pull too tightly. Finish on the inside between the body and the first arm. Tie off with the tail of the original thread.

making hairstyle 2

Take your doll. Mark position of eyes with pins. Insert pins along line of parting. Attach yarn to the first pin and then pull down to the bottom edge of the hair, securing with another pin. Bring the yarn back up to the parting and wrap around the pin before wrapping it again at the bottom edge. Continue wrapping the yarn around pins between the parting and bottom of hair until half the head is well covered, adding more pins around the bottom as you go. İf necessary you can wrap yarn around the same pins a few times. Using sewing thread, sew the hair in place along the parting with small stitches, then sew along the bottom edge to secure hair. Continue in this way to complete the other side of the hair, then remove pins. To make braids, cut yarn into 2 bundles of 12in (30cm) lengths. Tie a knot at the middle of each bunch. Weave braids and tie with yarn to secure. Sew onto the head and trim ends.

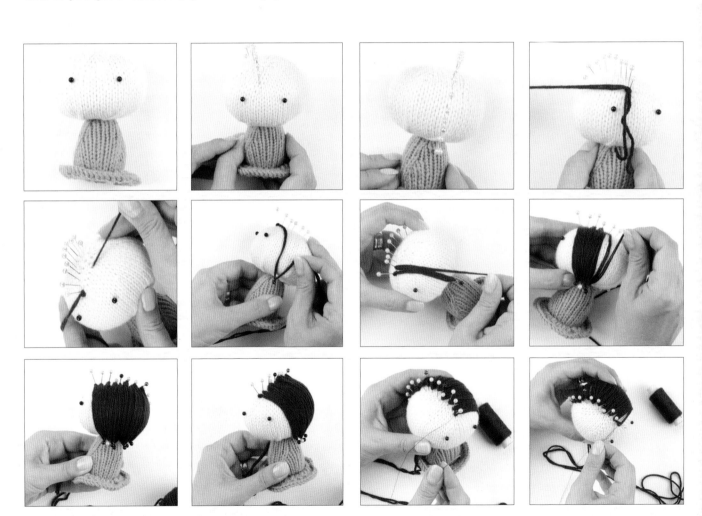

32

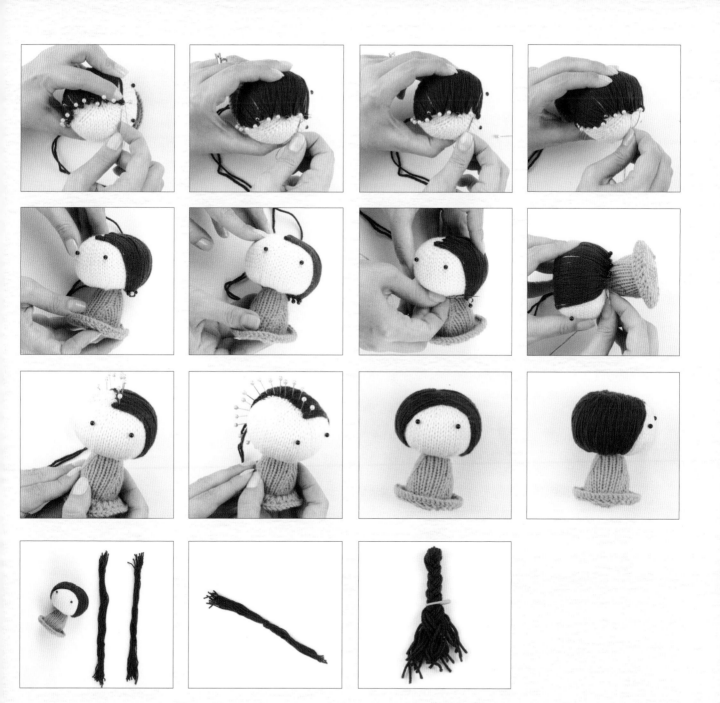

wire legs

Cut 45 cm (17.8 inches) of thin wire (2mm). Insert the wire through the bottom of the body so that the centre point of the wire is inside the doll then bend gently in half so that the wire is pointing downwards. Then bend the wire back on itself to form each leg, inserting the ends inside the body. Knot the yarn to the wire. Secure thread and snip off the excess yarn end. Apply glue to the top of the leg. Wrap green yarn around the wire.

Apply glue to the end of the leg for fixing yarn. Thread your needle and then pul a knol al the end. Secure with little stitches at the 'toe' end of the leg. Continue wrapping with yarn, traveling back up to the top of the leg. Fix yarn on the top part with crochet hook and tie a knot. Hide the end inside of the body. Snip off the excess yarn. Bend to shape the foot. Repeat for the second leg.

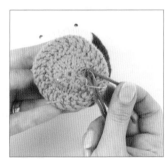

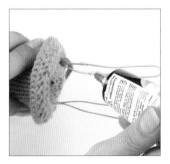

hair

Take your doll and temporarily position hood to help define the area for the face. Mark position of eyes and edges of face with pins. Thread needle with yarn and start off by inserting into back of head and out through the hole formed by the magic ring at the top, hiding the end inside the head as you do so. Insert needle at point where hair is to end and bring it back out of one knitted stitch along to the side, making a strand of hair with one long stitch. Then insert the needle in at edge of ring at top, bringing it out again at the hole. Continue stitching in this way, gradually building up strands of hair until you have covered all around the face. Continue around the back if this area will be seen, or simply reposition the hood and secure.

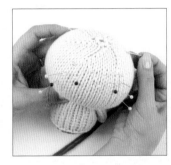

Projects

Coral Doll With Small Bear Named Lin

ABBREVIATIONS

CO cast on
DPN(s) double pointed needle(s)
K knit
K2tog knit 2 together
Kfb knit into front and
back of stitch
P purl
RND round
st(s) stitch(es)
YO yarn over

MATERIALS NEEDED

• US 2½ (3mm) 4 double-pointed
needles
• Crochet hook of similar size to
needles
• DMC Natura Just Cotton
50g/155m
Colors: 1 ball each of Coral (N18)
and Lin (N78)
• DMC Woolly yarn 50g/125m balls
Colors: 1 ball each of
        white (01)
        blue (075)
• Toy Stuffing
• Tapestry needle
• Stitch marker
• 2 pairs of black beads (4mm)
• Plastic nose
• Glue
• Flexible aluminium wire (2mm
thick)
• Pink Blush

NOTES

**Finished doll is approximately 8.6"
(22 cm) tall.**

**Gauge (tension) is not critical, but
when knitting toys the knitted fabric
should be worked fairly tightly to
ensure a dense fabric that will hold
the stuffing in. If you are a loose
knitter you may wish to use smaller
needles than size stated.**

**See page 22 for how to make
magic rings.**

See page 24 for how to knit I-cord

BODY

Body and head are made in one
piece .

Using white yarn (color 01) with two
threads held together make a closed
magic ring of 6 sts.

Distribute sts across 3 DPNs, place
marker and begin working in rounds.

RND1: Kfb 6 times. (12 sts)
RND2: (Kfb, K1) 6 times. (18 sts)

RND3: (Kfb, K2) 6 times. (24 sts)
RND4: (Kfb, K3) 6 times. (30 sts)
RND5: (Kfb, K4) 6 times. (36 sts)
RND6-16: Knit 11 Rnds.
RND17: (K2tog, K4) 6 times. (30 sts)
RND18: K2tog 15 times. (15 sts)
RND19: (K2tog, K3) 3 times. (12 sts)
RND20: K2tog 6 times. (6 sts)
RND21: Kfb 6 times. (12 sts)
RND22: Kfb 12 times. (24 sts)
RND23-25: Knit 3 rnds.
RND26: (Kfb, K3) 6 times. (30 sts)
RND27-37: Knit 11 rnds.
RND38: (K2tog, K3) 6 times. (24 sts)
Continue to work decrease rnds,
adding stuffing as you go.
RND39: (K2tog, K2) 6 times. (18 sts)
RND40: (K2tog, K1) 6 times. (12 sts)
RND41: K2tog 6 times. (6 sts)

Cut yarn and thread through 6 remaining sts (adding more stuffing if
required), pull to tighten and secure.

Weave in ends.

LEGS (make 2)

Using white yarn (color 01) with two
threads held together CO 8sts.

Distribute sts across 3 DPNs. Place marker and join for working in the round, being careful not to twist cast on edge.

RND1-35: Knit 35 rnds. (8 sts)
Change to blue yarn (color 075).
RND36: Kfb 8 times. (16 sts)
RND37: (Kfb, K1) 4 times, K8. (20 sts)
RND38-41: Knit 4 rnds.
RND42: Purl.
RND43: Knit.
RND44: (K2tog, K1) 4 times, K8. (16 sts)
RND45: Knit.

Continue to work decrease rounds, adding stuffing as you go.

RND46: K2tog 8 times. (8 sts)
RND47: K2tog 4 times. (4 sts)

Cut yarn and thread through remaining 4 sts (adding more stuffing if required), pull to tighten and secure.

Weave in ends.

ARMS (make2)
Using white yarn (color 01) with two threads held together make a closed magic ring of 7 sts.

Distribute sts across 3 DPNs, place marker and begin working in rounds.

RND1-18: Knit 18 rnds. (7 sts)
RND19: Kfb, K6. (8 sts)
RND20-22: Knit 3 rnds. (8 sts)

SHAPING FINGERS

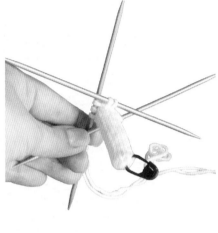

Fingers are worked on 2 sts at a time.

Work with the first 2 sts, knitting as for i-cord.

RND23-25: Knit 3 rnds. (2 sts)

Cut yarn and thread through remaining 2 sts, pull to tighten and secure.

Weave in ends.

Repeat process above for remaining 3 fingers.

DRESS

Using Coral yarn (color 18) CO 36 sts.

Distribute sts across 3 DPNs. Place marker and join for working in the round, being careful not to twist cast on edge.

RND1-2: Knit 2 rnds.
Change to Lin yarn (color 78).

RND3: Kfb 36 times. (72 sts)

Change to Coral yarn (color 18).
RND4-10: Knit 7 rnds. (72 sts)
RND11: (K2tog, YO) 36 times.
RND12: Knit.
RND13 - 16: As RND11-12.
RND17: As RND11.

Bind off.

STRAPS OF DRESS (make 2)

Knitted flat.
Using Coral yarn (color 18) CO 6 sts.

RND1: Knit.
RND2: Kfb 6 times. (12 sts)
RND3: Kfb 12 times. (24 sts)
RND4: Purl.
RND5: (K2tog, YO) 12 times. (24 sts)
RND6: Purl.

Bind off.

GAITERS (make 2)

Using Coral yarn (color 18) CO 12 sts.

Distribute sts across 3 DPNs. Place marker and join for working in the round, being careful not to twist cast on edge.

Change to Lin yarn (color 78).
RND1: Knit.

Change to Coral yarn (color 18).
RND2: Knit.
These 2 rnds set stripe pattern.
RND3-8: Work stripes as set for a further 6 rnds.

Bind off.

ASSEMBLING AND FINISHING
1. Knit all the parts.
2. Shaping feet: To make the feet flatter on the base, take a long piece of yarn, and thread it on your needle and knot it on one end. Starting at the underside of the sole, push your needle out through the top of the foot .Taking a small stitch, go back through the foot to the outside of sole. Repeat this process one or two more times, gently pulling the thread to tighten the foot with each pass and being careful not to indent too deeply. Secure thread and snip off the excess yarn.
3. Position the gaiters on the legs.
4. Sew legs to the body.
5. Sew the arms to the body.
6. With yarn to match, sew running stitch along the top edge of dress. Pull to tighten and before fastening try it on the doll to check fit. Adjust it to fit the doll's underarm line, fasten off yarn and weave in end.
7. Position straps and sew them to the gather line of dress.
8. Hairstyle, Pierce the wire through the head into the place where you want to make the pony tails. Using Coral yarn (color N51), knot the yarn to the wire. Wrap from one side of the head to the other catching around the wire. When the head is completely covered start to make the pony tails. Wrap yarn around the wire until it is half covered with yarn. Bend the wire before continuing to wrap. Thread the needle and secure the ponytails with little stitches around the wire. Continue to wrap around the wire until it is completely covered with yarn. I kept going until it was quite thick. Finally secure the hair down onto the head with little stitches.
9. Sew beads for eyes.
10. Apply pink blush to cheeks.

BEAR NAMED LIN

BODY

Body and head are made in one piece.

Using Lin (color 78) with two threads held together make a closed magic ring of 6 sts.

Distribute sts across 3 DPNs, place marker and begin working in rnds.

RND1: Kfb 6 times. (12 sts)
RND2: (Kfb, K1) 6 times. (18 sts)
RND3: (Kfb, K2) 6 times. (24 sts)
RND4-10: Knit 7 rnds. (24 sts)
RND11: (K2tog, K2) 6 times. (18 sts)

Continue to work decrease rounds, adding stuffing as you go.

RND12: (K2tog, K1) 6 times. (12 sts)
RND13: K2tog 6 times. (6 sts)
RND14: (Kfb, K1) 3 times. (9 sts)
RND15: Knit.
RND16: (Kfb, K2) 3 times. (12 sts)
RND17-19: Knit 3 rnds.
RND20: (Kfb, K3) 3 times. (15 sts)
RND21: Knit.
RND22: (Kfb, K4) 3 times. (18 sts)

RND23-24: Knit 2 rnds.
RND25: (K2tog, K1) 6 times. (12 sts)
RND26: K2tog 6 times. (6 sts)

Cut yarn and thread through remaining 6 sts (adding more stuffing if required), pull to tighten and secure.

Weave in ends.

ARMS (make 2)
Using Lin (color 78) with two threads held together CO 4 sts.

Knit as for i-cord.
RND1-5: Knit 5 rnds.

Do not stuff.

Cut yarn and thread through remaining 4 sts, pull to tighten and secure.

Weave in ends.

LEGS (make 2)
Using Lin (color 78) with two threads held together CO 4 sts.

Knit as for i-cord.

RND1-4: Knit 4 rnds.

Do not stuff.

Cut yarn and thread through remaining 4 sts, pull to tighten and secure.

Weave in ends.

EARS (make 2)

Using Lin (color 78) with two threads held together make a closed magic ring of 6 sts.

Distribute sts across 3 DPNs, place marker and begin working in rnds.

RND1: Kfb 6 times. (12 sts)
RND2: Purl.
RND3: K2tog 6 times. (6 sts)

Cut yarn and thread through remaining 6 sts, pull to tighten and secure.

Weave in ends.

ASSEMBLING AND FINISHING
1. Knit all the parts.
2. Sew the arms and the legs to the body.
3. For best shaping of head and body wrap yarn around neck, make loop and pull thread as tight as you can. Secure and snip off the excess yarn.
4. Glue the plastic nose in place.
5. Sew beads for eyes.
6. Sew the ears to the head.
7. With sewing thread embroider small cross on the body.

Red Hood Doll

ABBREVIATIONS

Beg begin
CO cast on
DPN(s) double pointed needle(s)
K knit
K2tog knit 2 together
Kfb knit into front and back of stitch
P purl
RND round
sts stitches
st st stockinette stitch (knit all odd-numbered rows, purl all even numbered rows)
w&t wrap and turn

MATERIALS NEEDED

• US 2½ (3mm) 4 double-pointed needles
• Crochet hook of similar size to needles
• **DMC Woolly yarn 50g/125m balls**
Colors: 2 balls of
        white (01)
1 ball each of
        black (02)
        red (052)
• Toy stuffing
• Tapestry needle
• Stitch marker
• 1 pair of black plastic eyes (10mm half beads)
• Pink ribbon
• Crochet hook
• Glue
• Pink blush

NOTES

Finished doll is approximately 9" (23 cm) tall.

Gauge (tension) is not critical, but when knitting toys the knitted fabric should be worked fairly tightly to ensure a dense fabric that will hold the stuffing in. If you are a loose knitter you may wish to use smaller needles than size stated.

See page 22 for how to make open or closed magic ring.

See page 24 for how to knit I-cord

HEAD

Using white yarn (color 01) with two threads held together make an open magic ring of 6 sts.

Distribute sts across 3 DPNs, place marker and begin working in rounds.

RND1: Kfb 6 times. (12 sts)
RND2: (Kfb, K1) 6 times. (18 sts)
RND3: (Kfb, K2) 6 times. (24 sts)
RND4: (Kfb, K3) 6 times. (30 sts)
RND5: (Kfb, K4) 6 times. (36 sts)

RND6: (Kfb, K5) 6 times. (42 sts)
RND7: (Kfb, K6) 6 times. (48 sts)
RND8-23: Knit 16 rnds.
RND24: (K2tog, K6) 6 times. (2 sts)
RND25: (K2tog, K5) 6 times. (36 sts)
RND26: (K2tog, K4) 6 times. (30 sts)
RND27: (K2tog, K3) 6 times. (24 sts)

Continue to work decrease rounds, adding stuffing as you go.

RND28: (K2tog, K2) 6 times. (18 sts)
RND29: (K2tog, K1) 6 times. (12 sts)
RND30: K2tog 6 times. (6 sts)

Cut yarn and thread through remaining 6 sts (adding more stuffing if required). Pull to tighten and secure, leaving a small hole for sewing the head to the body.

Weave in ends.

BODY

Starting at the bottom of the body, using white yarn (color 01) with two threads held together make an open magic ring of 6 sts.

Distribute sts across 3 DPNs, place

marker and begin working in rounds.

RND1: Kfb 6 times. (12 sts)
RND2: (Kfb, K1) 6 times. (18 sts)
RND3: (Kfb, K2) 6 times. (24 sts)
RND4: (Kfb, K3) 6 times. (30 sts)
RND5: Purl.
RND6-8: Knit 3 rnds.
RND9: (K2tog, K8) 3 times. (27 sts)
RND10: Knit.
RND11: (K2tog, K7) 3 times. (24 sts)
RND12: Knit.
RND13: (K2tog, K6) 3 times. (21 sts)
RND14-15: Knit 2 rnds.
RND16: (K2tog, K5) 3 times. (18 sts)
RND17-18: Knit 2 rnds.
RND19: (K2tog, K4) 3 times. (15 sts)
RND20-21: Knit 2 rnds.
RND22: (K2tog, K3) 3 times. (12 sts)

Work decrease rounds, adding stuffing as you go.

RND23-25: Knit 3 rnds.
RND26: (K2tog, K2) 3 times. (9 sts)
RND27-29: Knit 3 rnds.

Cut yarn and thread through remaining 9 sts (adding more stuffing if required). Pull to tighten and secure, leaving a small hole for sewing the head to the body.

Weave in ends.

DRESS RUFFLE

Using white yarn (color 01) with one thread only, pick up and knit 30 sts along purl bumps from RND5 of the body.

Place marker and begin working in rnds.

RND1: Kfb 30 times. (60 sts)
RND2: (Kfb, K1) 30 times. (90 sts)
RND3-8: Knit 6 rnds.
RND9: Purl.

Bind off

COAT

Using red yarn (color 052) with two threads held together CO 18 sts.

Knitted flat.

Row 1: Knit.
Row 2: K2. P to last 2 sts, K2.
Row 3: K6. Kfb, K to last 7 sts, Kfb, K6. (20 sts)
Row 4-17: Rep rows 2-3 a further 7 times. (32 sts)
Row 18: (Kfb, K1) 17 times. (51 sts)
Row 19: Knit.
Row 20: (Kfb, K2) 17 times. (68 sts)
Row 21-25: Knit 5 rows.

Change to white yarn (color 01).

Bind off.

HOOD

Using red yarn (color 052) with two threads held together make a closed magic ring of 6 sts.

Distribute sts across 3 DPNs, place marker and begin working in rounds.

RND 1: Kfb 6 times. (12 sts)
RND 2: (Kfb, K1) 6 times. (18 sts)
RND 3: (Kfb, K2) 6 times. (24 sts)
RND 4: (Kfb, K3) 6 times. (30 sts)
RND 5: (Kfb, K4) 6 times. (36 sts)
RND 6: (Kfb, K5) 6 times. (42 sts)
RND 7: (Kfb, K6) 6 times. (48 sts)
RND 8: (Kfb, K7) 6 times. (54 sts)
RND 9: (Kfb, K8) 6 times. (60 sts)
RND 10: (Kfb, K9) 6 times. (66 sts)
RND 11: (Kfb, K10) 6 times. (72 sts)
RND 12-25: Knit 14 rnds.

Beg working flat.

Turn work to the wrong side.

Row 26: Purl.
Row 27: K1, Kfb, K68, Kfb, K1. (74sts)
Row 28-32: Beg with a purl row work 5 rows in st st.
Row 33-37: Knit 5 rows.

Change to white yarn (color 01).

Bind off.

ARMS (make 2)

Using white yarn (color 01) with two threads held together CO 4 sts.

Knit as for i-cord.

RND1-20: Knit 20 rnds.

Do not stuff.

Cut yarn and thread through remaining 4 sts, pull to tighten and secure.

Weave in ends.

SLEEVES (make 2)

Using red yarn (color 052) with two threads held together make a closed magic ring of 6 sts.

Distribute sts across 3 DPNs, place marker and begin working in rounds.

RND 1-13: Knit.

RND 14: (Kfb, K1) 3 times. (9 sts)
RND 15-17: Knit 3 rnds.
RND 18: Purl.

Change to white yarn (color 01).
RND 19-21: Beg with a knit row work 3 rows in st st.

Bind off.

SOCKS (make 2)

Using white yarn (color 01) with two threads held together CO 7 sts.

Distribute sts across 3 DPNs. Place marker and join for working in the round, being careful not to twist cast on edge.

RND 1-4: Knit 4 rnds.
Change to black yarn (color 02).
RND 5-7: Knit 3 rnds.

Change to white yarn (color 01).
RND 8-10: Knit 3 rnds.

RND 11-28: Rnds 5-10 set stripe pattern. Continue to works stripes as set for a further 18 rnds.

Change to black yarn (color 02).

RND 29-34: Knit 6 rnds.

Beg knitting short rows:

RND 35: K4, w&t, P3, w&t, K6. (7 sts)
RND 36: Knit.
RND 37: K4, w&t, P3, w&t, K6. (7 sts)
RND 38-39: Knit 2 rnds.

Place a small amount of stuffing into the foot only, do not stuff the legs.

Cut yarn and thread through remaining 7 sts, pull to tighten and secure.

Weave in ends.

HAIR

Using black yarn (color 02) with two threads held together make a closed magic ring of 6 sts.

Distribute sts across 3 DPNs, place marker and begin working in rounds.

RND 1: Kfb 6 times. (12 sts)
RND 2: (Kfb, K1) 6 times. (18 sts)
RND 3: (Kfb, K2) 6 times. (24 sts)
RND 4: (Kfb, K3) 6 times. (30 sts)
RND 5: (Kfb, K4) 6 times. (36 sts)

RND 6: (Kfb, K5) 6 times. (42 sts)
RND 7: (Kfb, K6) 6 times. (48 sts)
RND 8: (Kfb, K15) 3 times. (51 sts)
RND 9-15: Knit 7 rnds.
RND 16: P17, K to end. (51 sts)

Shaping bangs.

RND 17: Bind off 16sts, K to end. (35 sts)

Begin working flat.

Turn work to the wrong side.

Row 18-21: Beg with a purl row work 4 rows in st st.
Row 22: P2tog, P to end. (34 sts)
Row 23: (K7, K2tog) 3 times, K7. (31 sts)
Row 24: Purl.
Row 25: (K6, K2tog) 3 times, K7. (28 sts)
Row 26: Purl.
Row 27: K21, w&t, P14, w&t, K21. (28 sts)
Row 28: Purl.
Row 29: (K5, K2tog) 4 times. (24 sts)

Bind off.

BUNS (make 2)
Each bun consists of two parts: ball and cord.

Ball
Using black yarn (color 02) with two threads held together make a closed magic ring of 6 sts.

Distribute sts across 3 DPNs, place marker and begin working in rounds.

RND 1: Kfb 6 times. (12 sts)

RND 2: (Kfb, K3) 3 times. (15 sts)
RND 3-4: Knit 2 rnds.

Work decrease rounds, adding stuffing as you go.

RND 5: (K2tog, K3) 3 times. (12 sts)
RND 6: K2tog 6 times. (6 sts)

Cut yarn and thread through 6 remaining sts (adding more stuffing if required).

Pull to tighten and secure, leaving small hole for ribbon.

Weave in ends.

Cord
Using black yarn (color 02) with two threads held together CO 4 sts.

Knit as for i-cord.
RND 1-60: Knit 60 rnds.

Do not stuff.

Cut yarn and thread through remaining 4 sts, pull to tighten and secure.

Weave in ends.

ASSEMBLING AND FINISHING
1. Knit all the parts.
2. Sew the head onto the body.
3. Insert the arms into the sleeves. I used a crochet hook for this.
4. Position the coat on the body and secure it with pins.
5. Sew the arms to the body.
6. Sew legs to the bottom of the body.
7. Position the hood on the head and sew along the neck line of coat.
8. Position the hair onto the head and secure it with pins, then sew to secure.
9. Finish each bun: roll up the cord in a spiral and sew through all rings to secure. Take the ball and using the crochet hook pass two ribbons held together through the ball. Sew the ball to the middle of spiral.
10. Sew the buns to the hair.
11. Glue the plastic eyes into place.
12. Apply pink blush to cheeks.

Iris Doll

ABBREVIATIONS

Beg begin
CO cast on
DPN(s) double pointed needle(s)
K knit
K2tog knit 2 together
Kfb knit into front and back of stitch
P purl
RND round
st(s) stitch(es)
st st stockinette stitch (knit all odd numbered rows, purl all even numbered rows)
w&t wrap and turn

MATERIALS NEEDED

• US 2½ (3mm) 4 double-pointed needles
• Crochet hook of similar size to needles
• **DMC Woolly yarn 50g/125m**
Colors: 1 ball each of
      white (01)
      black (02)
      cream (03)
      lilac (062)
      violet (065)
      green (074)
• Toy Stuffing
• Tapestry needle
• Stitch marker
• 1 pair of black plastic eyes (6mm half beads)
• Glue
• Pink blush

NOTES

Finished doll is approximately 9" (23 cm) tall.

Gauge (tension) is not critical, but when knitting toys the knitted fabric should be worked fairly tightly to ensure a dense fabric that will hold the stuffing in. If you are a loose knitter you may wish to use smaller needles than size stated.

See page 22 for how to make magic rings.

See page 24 for how to knit I-cord.

See page 27 for how to knit short rows.

HEAD

Using cream yarn (color 03) make an open magic ring of 6 sts.

Distribute sts across 3 DPNs, place marker and begin working in rounds.

RND 1: Kfb 6 times. (12 sts)
RND 2: (Kfb, K1) 6 times. (18 sts)
RND 3: (Kfb, K2) 6 times. (24 sts)
RND 4: (Kfb, K3) 6 times. (30 sts)
RND 5: (Kfb, K4) 6 times. (36 sts)
RND 6: (Kfb, K5) 6 times. (42 sts)
RND 7-23: knit 17 rnds.
RND 24: (K2tog, K5) 6 times. (36 sts)
RND 25: (K2tog, K4) 6 times. (30 sts)
RND 26: (K2tog, K3) 6 times. (24 sts)

Continue to work decrease rounds, adding stuffing as you go.

RND 27: (K2tog, K2) 6 times. (18 sts)
RND 28: (K2tog, K1) 6 times. (12 sts)
RND 29: K2tog 6 times. (6 sts)

Cut yarn and thread through remaining 6 sts (adding more stuffing if required). Pull to tighten and secure, leaving a small hole for sewing the head to the body.

Weave in ends.

BODY

Starting at the bottom of the body and using lilac yarn (color 062), make an open magic ring of 6 sts.

Distribute sts across 3 DPNs, place marker and begin working in rounds.

RND 1: Kfb 6 times. (12 sts)
RND 2: (Kfb, K1) 6 times. (18 sts)
RND 3: (Kfb, K2) 6 times. (24 sts)
RND 4: (Kfb, K3) 6 times. (30 sts)
RND 5: Purl.
RND 6-7: Knit 2 rnds.
RND 8: (K2tog, K8) 3 times. (27 sts)
RND 9: Knit.
RND 10: (K2tog, K7) 3 times. (24 sts)
RND 11: Knit.
RND 12: (K2tog, K6) 3 times. (21 sts)
RND 13-14: Knit 2 rnds.
RND 15: (K2tog, K5) 3 times. (18 sts)
RND 16-17: Knit 2 rnds.
RND 18: (K2tog, K4) 3 times. (15 sts)
RND 19-21: Knit 3 rnds.
RND 22: (K2tog, K3) 3 times. (12 sts)

Continue to work decrease rounds, adding stuffing as you go.

RND 23-25: Knit 3 rnds.
RND 26: (K2tog, K2) 3 times. (9 sts)
RND 27-29: Knit 3 rnds.
RND 30: (K2tog, K1) 3 times. (6 sts)

Cut yarn and thread through remaining 6 sts (adding more stuffing if required). Pull to tighten and secure, leaving a small hole for sewing the head to the body.

Weave in ends.

DRESS RUFFLE

Using lilac yarn (color 062) pick up and knit 30 sts along purl bumps from RND5 of the body.

Place marker and begin working in rnds.

RND 1: Kfb 30 times. (60 sts)
RND 2: (Kfb, K1) 30 times. (90 sts)
RND 3-7: Knit 5 rnds.

Bind off.

COAT
Using violet yarn (color 065) CO 20 sts.

Knitted flat.

Row 1: Knit.
Row 2: K3, P to end, K3.
Row 3: K5. Kfb, K to last 6 sts, Kfb, K5. (22 sts)
Row 4-17: Repeat rows 2-3 a further 7 times. (36 sts)
Row 18: (Kfb, K1) 18 times. (54 sts)
Row 19: Knit.
Row 20: (Kfb, K2) 18 times. (72 sts)
Row 21-24: Knit 4 rows.

Change to green yarn (color 074).

Row25-26: Knit 2 rows.

Bind off.

HOOD

Using violet yarn (color 065) make a closed magic ring of 6 sts.

Distribute sts across 3 DPNs, place marker and begin working in rounds.

RND 1: Kfb 6 times. (12 sts)
RND 2: (Kfb, K1) 6 times. (18 sts)
RND 3: (Kfb, K2) 6 times. (24 sts)
RND 4: (Kfb, K3) 6 times. (30 sts)
RND 5: (Kfb, K4) 6 times. (36 sts)
RND 6: (Kfb, K5) 6 times. (42 sts)
RND 7: (Kfb, K6) 6 times. (48 sts)
RND 8: (Kfb, K7) 6 times. (54 sts)
RND 9: (Kfb, K8) 6 times. (60 sts)
RND 10: (Kfb, K9) 6 times. (66 sts)
RND 11: (Kfb, K10) 6 times. (72 sts)
RND 12-23: Knit 12 rnds.

Begin working flat.

Turn work to the wrong side.

Row 24: Purl.
Row 25: Knit.
Row 26: K1, Kfb, Kto last 2 sts, Kfb, K1. (74 sts)
Row 27-30: Knit 4 rows.

Change to green (color 074).

Row 31: K2tog, K to end, K2tog. (72 sts)

Row 32-34: Repeat row 31 a further 3 times. (66 sts)

Bind off.

ARMS (make 2)

Using cream yarn (color 03) CO 4 sts.

Knit as for i-cord.

RND 1-20: Knit 20 rnds.

Do not stuff.

Cut yarn and thread through remaining 4 sts, pull to tighten and secure.

Weave in ends.

SLEEVES (make 2)

Using violet yarn (color 065) make a closed magic ring of 6 sts.

Distribute sts across 3 DPNs, place marker and begin working in rounds.

RND 1-13: Knit.
RND 14: (Kfb, K1) 3 times. (9 sts)
RND 15-17: Knit 3 rnds.
RND 18-21: Beg with a purl row work 4 rows in st st.

Bind off.

SOCKS (make 2)

Using white yarn (color 01) CO 6 sts.

Distribute sts across 3 DPNs. Place marker and join for working in the round, being careful not to twist cast on edge.

RND 1-4: Knit 4 rnds.

Change to black yarn (color 02).
RND 5-7: Knit 3 rnds.

Change to white yarn (color 01).
RND 8-10: Knit 3 rnds.
RND 11-29: Rnds 5-10 set stripe pattern. Continue to work stripes as set.

Change color to black.

RND 29-32: Knit 4 rows

Beg knitting short rows:

RND 33: K4, w&t, P3, w&t, K6. (6 sts)
RND 34: Knit.
RND 35: K4, w&t, P3, w&t , K6.
(6 sts)
RND 36-37: Knit 2 rnds.

Place a small amount of stuffing into the foot only, do not stuff the legs.

Cut yarn and thread through remaining 6 sts, pull to tighten and secure.

Weave in ends.

ASSEMBLING AND FINISHING
1. Knit all the parts.
2. Sew the head onto the body.
3. Insert the arms into the sleeves. I used a crochet hook for this.
4. Position the coat on the body and secure it with pins.
5. Sew the arms to the body.
6. Sew legs to the bottom of the body.
7. Embroider the dolls hair using black yarn (color 02).
8. Position the hood on the head and sew along the neck line of coat.
9. Glue the plastic eyes into place.
10. Apply pink blush to cheeks.

Tiger
Tanoshi Doll

64

ABBREVIATIONS

Beg begin
CO cast on
DPN(s) double pointed needle(s)
K knit
K2tog knit 2 together
K3tog knit 3 together
Kfb knit into front and back of stitch
P purl
RND round
sts stitches
st st stockinette stitch (knit all odd numbered rows, purl all even numbered rows)

MATERIALS NEEDED

- US 6 (4 mm) 4 double-pointed needles.
- Crochet hook of similar size to needles
- **DMC Natura Just Cotton XL yarn 100g/75m**
Colors: 1 ball each of
cream (03)
orange (10)
navy (71)
- Toy Stuffing
- Tapestry needle
- Stitch marker
- 1 pair of black buttons (10 mm)
- Orange blush

NOTES

Finished doll is approximately 7" (18 cm) tall.

Gauge (tension) is not critical, but when knitting toys the knitted fabric should be worked fairly tightly to ensure a dense fabric that will hold the stuffing in. If you are a loose knitter you may wish to use smaller needles than size stated.

See page 22 for how to make open or closed magic ring.

HEAD

Using cream yarn (color 03) make an open magic ring of 6 sts.

Distribute sts across 3 DPNs, place marker and begin working in rounds.

RND 1: Kfb 6 times. (12 sts)
RND 2: (Kfb, K1) 6 times. (18 sts)
RND 3: (Kfb, K2) 6 times. (24 sts)
RND 4: (Kfb, K3) 6 times. (30 sts)
RND 5: (Kfb, K4) 6 times. (36 sts)
RND 6: (Kfb, K5) 6 times. (42 sts)
RND 7: (Kfb, K6) 6 times. (48 sts)
RND 8-21: Knit 14 rnds.
RND 22: (K2tog, K6) 6 times. (42 sts)

RND 23: (K2tog, K5) 6 times. (36 sts)
RND 24: (K2tog, K4) 6 times. (30 sts)
RND 25: (K2tog, K3) 6 times. (24 sts)

Continue to work decrease rounds, adding stuffing as you go.

RND 26: (K2tog, K2) 6 times. (18 sts)
RND 27: (K2tog, K1) 6 times. (12 sts)
RND 28: K2tog 6 times. (6 sts)

Cut yarn and thread through remaining 6 sts (adding more stuffing if required). Pull to tighten and secure, leaving a small hole for sewing the head to the body.

Weave in ends.

BODY

Using orange yarn (color 10) make an open magic ring of 6 sts.

Distribute sts across 3 DPNs, place marker and begin working in rounds.

RND 1: Kfb 6 times. (12 sts)
RND 2: (Kfb, K1) 6 times. (18 sts)
RND 3: (Kfb, K7, Kfb) twice. (22 sts)

RND 4: (Kfb, K9, Kfb) twice. (26 sts)
RND 5: Purl.
RND 6-8: Knit 3 rnds.
RND 9: (K2tog, K9, K2tog) twice. (22 sts)
RND 10-12: Knit 3 rnds.
RND 13: (K2tog, K7, K2tog) twice. (18 sts)
RND 14-16: Knit 3 rnds.
RND 17: (K2tog, K5, K2tog) twice. (14 sts)
RND 18-21: Knit 4 rnds.

Continue to work decrease rounds, adding stuffing as you go.

RND 22: (K2tog, K3, K2tog) twice. (10 sts)
RND 23-24: Knit.
RND 25: (K2tog, K1, K2tog) twice. (6 sts)

Cut yarn and thread through remaining 6 sts (adding more stuffing if required). Pull to tighten and secure, leaving a small hole for sewing the head to the body.

Weave in ends.

HOOD

Using orange yarn (color 10) make a closed magic ring of 6 sts.

Distribute sts across 3 DPNs, place marker and begin working in rounds.

RND 1: Kfb 6 times. (12 sts)
RND 2: (Kfb, K1) 6 times. (18 sts)
RND 3: (Kfb, K2) 6 times. (24 sts)
RND 4: (Kfb, K3) 6 times. (30 sts)
RND 5: (Kfb, K4) 6 times. (36 sts)
RND 6: (Kfb, K5) 6 times. (42 sts)
RND 7: (Kfb, K6) 6 times. (48 sts)
RND 8: (Kfb, K7) 6 times. (54 sts)
RND 9-22: Knit 14 rnds.

Beg working flat.

Turn work to the wrong side.

Row 23: P2tog, P to last 2 sts, P2tog. (52 sts)

Change to navy yarn (color 71).
Row 24: K2tog, K to last 2 sts, K2tog. (50 sts)

Change to orange yarn (color 10).
Row 25: K2tog, K15, K2tog, K14, K2tog, K15. (47 sts)

Change to navy yarn (color 71).
Row 26: Knit.

Change to orange yarn (color 10).
Row 27: K2tog, K14, K2tog, K13, K2tog, K14. (44 sts)

Change to navy yarn (color 71).
Row 28: K13, K2tog, K14, K2tog, K13. (42 sts)
Change to orange yarn (color 10).

Bind off.

ARMS (make 2)

Using orange yarn (color 10) make a closed magic ring of 5 sts.

Distribute sts across 3 DPNs, place marker and begin working in rounds.

RND 1-2: Knit 2 rnds.

Change to navy yarn (color 71).
RND 3: Knit.

Change to orange yarn (color 10).
RND 4: Knit.
RND 5-10: Rnds 3-4 set stripe pattern. Continue to work stripes as set for a further 6 rnds.

Do not stuff.

Cut yarn and thread through remaining 5 sts, pull to tighten and secure.

Weave in ends.

EARS (make 2)
Using orange yarn (color 10) CO 6 sts.

Distribute sts across 3 DPNs. Place marker and join for working in the round, being careful not to twist cast on edge.

RND 1-5: Knit 5 rnds.
RND 6: (K2tog, K5, K2tog) twice. (14 sts)
RND 7: Knit.
RND 8: (K2tog, K3, K2tog) twice. (10 sts)
RND 9: Knit.
RND 10: (K2tog, K1, K2tog) twice. (6 sts)

RND 11: Knit.
RND 12: K3tog twice. (2 sts)

Do not stuff.

Cut yarn and thread through remaining 2 sts, pull to tighten and secure.

Weave in ends

INNER EARS AND TUMMY (make 3)
Using cream yarn (color 03) CO 7 sts.

Knitted flat.

Row 1-4: Beg with a knit row work 4 rows in st st.
Row 5: K2tog, K3, K2tog. (5 sts)
Row 6: Purl.
Row 7: K2tog, K1, K2tog. (3 sts)
Row 8: Purl.
Row 9: K3tog. (1 st)

Fasten off.

TAIL

Using orange yarn (color 10) CO 7 stitches.

Distribute sts across 3 DPNs. Place marker and join for working in the round, being careful not to twist cast on edge.
RND 1-4: Knit 4 rnds.

Change to navy yarn (color 71).
RND 5-6: Knit 2 rnds.

Change to orange yarn (color 10).
RND 7-9: Knit 3 rnds.
RND 10-24: Rnds 5-9 set stripe pattern. Continue to work stripes as set for a further 15 rnds.

Change to navy yarn (color 71).
RND 25: K5, K2tog. (6 sts)
RND 26-30: Knit 5 rnds.
RND 31: K2tog 3 times. (3 sts)

Do not stuff.

Cut yarn and thread through remaining 3 sts, pull to tighten and secure.

Weave in ends

ASSEMBLING AND FINISHING

1. Knit all the parts.

2. Sew the head onto the body.

3. Sew the arms to the body.

4. Embroider the dolls hair using navy yarn (color 71).

5. Position the hood on the head and sew in place along the neck line.

6. Sew on buttons for eyes.

7. Sew inner ears to ears.

8. Sew tummy to the centre of the body.

9. Pin the ears and in place then sew them to the hood.

10. Apply orange blush to cheeks.

11. Sew the tail to the body.

12. Using navy yarn (color 71) embroider stripes on the body and hood.

Blue Doll
For Playtime

ABBREVIATIONS

CO cast on
DPN(s) double pointed needle(s)
K knit
K2tog knit 2 together
K3tog knit 3 together
Kfb knit into front and back of stitch
P purl
RND round
sl1 wyif with yarn in front, slip 1 st purlwise.
Sts stitches

MATERIALS NEEDED

• US 2½ (3mm) 4 double-pointed needles.
• Crochet hook of similar size to needles
• **DMC Woolly yarns 50g/125m**
Colors: 1 ball of
    cream (03)
 2 balls of
    light green (073)
• Toy Stuffing
• Tapestry needle
• Stitch marker
• Stitch holder
• Pink blush

NOTES

Finished doll is approximately 8.6" (22 cm) tall.

Gauge (tension) is not critical, but when knitting toys the knitted fabric should be worked fairly tightly to ensure a dense fabric that will hold the stuffing in. If you are a loose knitter you may wish to use smaller needles than size stated.

See page 22 for how to make magic rings.

See page 26 for how to work in double knitting.

BODY

Body is made using the double knitting technique.

Using light green yarn (073) CO 64 sts.

Row 1-10: K1, sl1 wyif to end.
Row 11: K3tog, sl1 wyif (K1, sl1 wyif) to last 4 sts, K1, K3tog. (60 sts)
Row 12: K1, sl1 wyif to end.
Row 13-20: Repeat Rows 11-12 a further 4 times. (44 sts)

Row 21: K3tog, sl1 wyif, (K1, sl1 wyif) to last 4 sts, K1, K3tog. (40 sts)
Row 22-24: (K1, sl1 wyif) to end.
Row 25-32: Repeat Rows 21-24 twice more. (32 sts)
Row 33: Kfb twice, (K1, sl1 wyif) to last 2 sts, Kfb twice. (36 sts)
Row 34: (K1, sl1 wyif) to end.
Row 35: Kfb twice, (K1, sl1 wyif) to last 2 sts, Kfb twice. (40 sts)
Row 36-38: (K1, sl1 wyif) to end.
Row 39-44: Repeat Rows 33-38 once more. (48 sts)

Row 45: Kfb twice, (K1, sl1 wyif) to last 2 sts, Kfb twice. (52 sts)
Row 46: (K1, sl1 wyif) to end.

DIVIDE FOR LEGS
RIGHT LEG

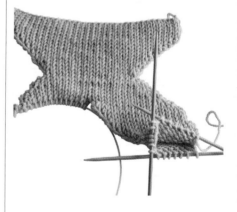

Row 47: (K1, sl1 wyif) 13 times, slip remaining 26 sts onto stitch holder or scrap yarn. (26sts)
Row 48: (K1, sl1 wyif) 13 times.
Row 49: Kfb twice, (K1, sl1 wyif) 12 times. (28sts)
Row 50: (K1, sl1 wyif) 14 times.
Row 51: Kfb twice, (K1, sl1 wyif) 11 times, K1, K3tog. (28 sts)

Row 52: (K1, sl1 wyif) 14 times.
Row 53: (K1, sl1 wyif) 12 times, K1, K3tog. (26 sts)
Row 54: (K1, sl1 wyif) 13 times.
Row 55: Kfb twice, (K1, sl1 wyif) 12times. (28 sts)
Row 56: (K1, sl1 wyif) 14 times.
Row 57: (K1, sl1 wyif) 12 times, K1, K3tog. (26 sts)
Row 58: (K1, sl1 wyif) 13 times.
Row 59: (K1, sl1 wyif) 11 times, K1, K3tog. (24 sts)
Row 60-62: (K1, sl1 wyif) 12 times.
Row 63: Kfb twice, (K1, sl1 wyif) 9 times, K1, K3tog. (24 sts)
Row 64-66: (K1, sl1 wyif) 12 times.
Row 67: K2tog, (K1, sl1 wyif) 10 times, K2tog. (22 sts)
Row 68: (Sl1 wyif, K1) 11 times.
Row 69: K2tog, (sl1 wyif, K1) 9 times, K2tog. (20 sts)
Row 70-76: (K1, sl1 wyif) 12 times.

Remove all stitches from the needles. Separate the two layers and distribute across 3DPNs. From this hole fill with toy stuffing. Form hands by taking a length of yarn and wrapping tightly around the wrist, knot firmly to secure and hide the ends inside.

Place marker and begin working in the round.

RND 77: Knit.
RND 78: (K2tog, K8) twice. (18 sts)
RND 79: Knit.
RND 80: (K2tog, K1) 6 times. (12 sts)
RND 81-82: Knit 2 rnds.
RND 83: K2tog 6 times. (6 sts)

Stuff the foot part.

Cut yarn and thread through remaining 6 sts (adding more stuffing if required), pull to tighten and secure.

Weave in ends.

LEFT LEG

Slip remaining 26 sts back onto a needle. With the work facing so that the completed leg lies to the left of the needle, re-join yarn to begin knitting.

Row 47: (K1, sl1 wyif) 13 times.
Row 48-83: Repeat Row48-83 as given for right leg, completing to match.

HEAD

Using cream yarn (color 03) with two threads held together make a closed magic ring of 6 sts.

Distribute sts across 3 DPNs, place marker and begin working in rounds.

RND 1: Kfb 6 times. (12 sts)
RND 2: (Kfb, K1) 6 times. (18 sts)
RND 3: (Kfb, K2) 6 times. (24 sts)
RND 4: (Kfb, K3) 6 times. (30 sts)
RND 5: (Kfb, K4) 6 times. (36 sts)
RND 6: (Kfb, K5) 6 times. (42 sts)
RND 7-16: Knit 10 rnds.
RND 17: (K2tog, K5) 6 times. (36 sts)
RND 18: (K2tog, K4) 6 times. (30 sts)
RND 19: (K2tog, K3) 6 times. (24 sts)

Continue to work decrease rounds, adding stuffing as you go.

RND 20: (K2tog, K2) 6 times. (18 sts)
RND 21: (K2tog, K1) 6 times. (12 sts)
RND 22: K2tog 6 times. (6 sts)

Cut yarn and thread through remaining 6 sts (adding more stuffing if required), pull to tighten and secure.

Weave in ends.

HAT

Using light green yarn (073) CO 44 sts.

Distribute sts across 3 DPNs, place marker and join to work in rounds, being careful not to twist cast on edge.

RND 1-6: (K2, P2) 10 times.
RND 7-9: Knit 3 rnds.
RND 10: (K2tog, K20) twice. (42 sts)
RND 11-13: Knit 3 rnds.
RND 14: (K2tog, K5) 6 times. (36 sts)

RND 15-16: Knit 2 rnds.
RND 17: (K2tog, K4) 6 times. (30 sts)
RND 18-20: Knit 3 rnds.
RND 21: (K2tog, K3) 6 times. (24 sts)
RND 22-25: Knit 4 rnds.
RND 26: (K2tog, K2) 6 times. (18 sts)
RND 27-31: Knit 5 rnds.
RND 32: (K2tog, K1) 6 times. (12 sts)
RND 33-39: Knit 7 rnds.
RND 40: K2tog 6 times. (6 sts)
RND 41-44: Knit 4 rnds.
RND 45: K2tog 3 times. (3 sts)

Cut yarn and thread through remaining 3 sts, pull to tighten and secure.

Weave in ends.

ASSEMBLING AND FINISHING
1. Knit all the parts.
2. Sew the head onto the body.
3. Position the hat onto the head.
4. Apply pink blush to cheeks.

Cutie
Bear Doll

ABBREVIATIONS

K3tog knit 3 together
DPN(s) double pointed needle(s)
K knit
K2tog knit 2 together
Kfb knit into front and back of stitch
P purl
P2tog purl 2 together
RND round
sl1 wyif with yarn in front, slip 1 st purlwise.
st(s) stitch(es)
st st stockinette stitch (knit all odd numbered rows, purl all even numbered rows)
YO yarn over

MATERIALS NEEDED

• US 4 (3.5mm) double pointed needles
• US 6 (4 mm) needles.
• Crochet hook of similar size to needles
• **DMC Woolly yarn 50g/125m**
Colors: 2 balls of
             cream (03)
3 balls of
             brown (116)
1 ball of
             light blue (071)
• Toy Stuffing
• Tapestry needle
• Stitch marker
• Stitch holder
• 1 pair of glass eyes
• Plastic nose
• Glue

NOTES

Finished doll is approximately 16.5" (42 cm) tall.

Gauge (tension) is not critical, but when knitting toys the knitted fabric should be worked fairly tightly to ensure a dense fabric that will hold the stuffing in. If you are a loose knitter you may wish to use smaller needles than size stated.

See page 22 for how to make magic rings.

See page 26 for how to work in double knitting.

BODY

Body is made using the double knitting technique.

Using brown yarn (color 116), with two threads held together and US 6 (4mm) needles CO 108 sts.

Row 1-20: (K1, sl1 wyif) to end.
Row 21: K3tog, sl1 wyif, (K1, sl1 wyif) to last 4 sts, K1, K3tog. (104 sts)
Row 22: K2tog, (K1, sl1 wyif) to last 2 sts, K2tog. (102 sts)
Row 23: K3tog, (K1, sl1 wyif) to last 3 sts, K3tog. (98 sts)
Row 24: Sl1 wyif, (K1, sl1 wyif) to last

st, K1.
Row 25: K3tog, (K1, sl1 wyif) to last 3 sts, K3tog. (94 sts)
Row 26: K2tog, sl1 wyif, (K1, sl1 wyif) to last 3 sts, K1, K2tog. (92 sts)
Row 27: K3tog, sl1 wyif, (K1, sl1 wyif) to last 4 sts, K1, K3tog. (88 sts)
Row 28: K2tog, (K1, sl1 wyif) to last 2 sts, K2tog. (86 sts)
Row 29: K3tog, (K1, sl1 wyif) to last 3 sts, K3tog. (82 sts)
Row 30: Sl1 wyif, (K1, sl1 wyif) to last st, K1.
Row 31: K3tog, (K1, sl1 wyif) to last 3 sts, K3tog. (78 sts)
Row 32: Sl1 wyif, (K1, sl1 wyif) to last st, K1.
Row 33: K3tog, (K1, sl1 wyif) to last 3 sts, K3tog. (74 sts)
Row 34: sl1 wyif, (K1, sl1 wyif) to last st, K1.
Row 35: K3tog, (K1, sl1 wyif) to last 3 sts, K3tog. (70 sts)
Row 36: Sl1 wyif, (K1, sl1 wyif) to last st, K1.
Row 37: K3tog, (K1, sl1 wyif) to last 3 sts, K3tog. (66 sts)
Row 38: K2tog, sl1 wyif, (K1, sl1 wyif) to last 3 sts, K1, K2tog. (64 sts)
Row 39: K3tog, sl1 wyif, (K1, sl1 wyif) to last 4 sts, K1, K3tog. (60 sts)
Row 40: (K1, sl1 wyif) to end.
Row 41-48: Repeat Row39-40 four times more. (44 sts)
Row 49-50: (K1, sl1 wyif) to end.
Row 51: Kfb twice, (K1, sl1 wyif) to last 2 sts, Kfb twice. (48 sts)
Row 52: (K1, sl1 wyif) to end.
Row 53-54: Repeat Row 51-52 once more. (52 sts)
Row 55: Kfb twice, (K1, sl1 wyif) to last 2 sts, Kfb twice. (56 sts)

Row 56-58: (K1, sl1 wyif) to end.
Row 59-70: Repeat Rows 55-58 three times more. (68 sts)
Row 71: Kfb twice, (K1, sl1 wyif) to last 2 sts, Kfb twice. (72 sts)
Row 72-76: (K1, sl1 wyif) to end.
Row 77- 88: Repeat Rows 55-58 three times more. (84 sts)
Row 89: Kfb twice, (K1, sl1 wyif) to last 2 sts, Kfb twice. (88 sts)
Row 90-94: (K1, sl1 wyif) to end.
Row 95: Repeat Rows 89-94 once more (92 sts)

DIVIDE FOR LEGS
RIGHT LEG

Row 101: (K1, sl1 wyif) 23 times, slip remaining sts onto stitch holder or scrap yarn. (46sts)
Row 102: (K1, sl1 wyif) to end.
Row 103: Kfb twice, (K1, sl1 wyif) to last 4 sts, K1, K3tog.
Row 104: K3tog, sl1 wyif, (K1, sl1 wyif) to end. (44 sts)
Row 105: (K1, sl1 wyif) to last 4 sts, K1, K3tog. (42 sts)
Row 106: K3tog, sl1 wyif, (K1, sl1 wyif) to end. (40 sts)
Row 107: Kfb twice, (K1, sl1 wyif) to last 4 sts, K1, K3tog.
Row 108: K3tog, sl1 wyif, (K1, sl1 wyif) to end. (38 sts)
Row 109-110: (K1, sl1 wyif) to end.
Row 111: Kfb twice, (K1, sl1 wyif) to end. (40 sts)
Row 112: K2tog, (K1, sl1 wyif) to end. (39 sts)
Row 113: (K1, sl1 wyif) to last 3 sts, K1, K2tog. (38 sts)
Row 114: K2tog, (K1, sl1 wyif) to end. (37 sts)
Row 115: (K1, sl1 wyif) to last 3 sts,

K3tog. (35 sts)
Row 116: K3tog, (K1, sl1 wyif) to end. (33 sts)
Row 117: Kfb, sl1 wyif, (K1, sl1 wyif) to last 3 sts, K3tog. (32 sts)
Row 118: K3tog, (K1, sl1 wyif) to last st, K1. (30 sts)
Row 119: Sl1 wyif, (K1, sl1 wyif) to last 3 sts, K3tog. (28 sts)
Row 120: Sl1 wyif, (K1, sl1 wyif) to last st, K1.
Row 121: Kfb, (K1, sl1 wyif) to last 3 sts, K3tog. (27 sts)
Row 122: Sl1 wyif, (K1, sl1 wyif) to end.
Row 123: (K1, sl1 wyif) to last 3 sts, K3tog. (25 sts)
Row 124: Sl1 wyif, (K1, sl1 wyif) to end.
Row 125: Kfb, sl1 wyif, (K1, sl1 wyif) to last 3 sts, K3tog. (24 sts)
Row 126: K3tog, (K1, sl1 wyif) to last st, K1. (22 sts)
Row 127: Sl1 wyif, (K1, sl1 wyif) to last 3 sts, K3tog. (20 sts)
Row 128: K3tog, (K1, sl1 wyif) to last st, K1. (18 sts)
Row 129: Sl1 wyif, (K1, **sl1** wyif) to last 3 sts, K3tog. (16 sts)
Row 130: Sl1 wyif, (K1, sl1 wyif) to last st, K1.
Row 131: Kfb, (K1, sl1 wyif) to last 3 sts, K3tog. (15 sts)

Remove all stitches from the needles. Separate the two layers and distribute across 3DPNs.

From this hole fill with toy stuffing. Form hands by taking a length of yarn and wrapping tightly around the wrist, knot firmly to secure and hide the ends inside.

Place marker and begin working in the round.

RND 132-133: Knit 2 rnds.
RND 134: (K2tog, K3) 3 times. (12 sts)
RND 135: K2tog 6 times. (6 sts)

Stuff the foot part.

Cut yarn and thread through remaining 6 sts (adding more stuffing if required), pull to tighten and secure.

Weave in ends.

LEFT LEG

Slip remaining 46 sts back onto a needle. With the work facing so that the completed leg lies to the left of the needle, re-join yarn to begin knitting.

Row 101: (K1, sl1 wyif) to end. (46 sts)
Row 102-135: Repeat Rows 102-135 as given above for right leg, completing to match.

HEAD

With cream yarn (color 03), two threads held together, and using US 4 (3.5mm) needles, make a closed magic ring of 6 sts.

Distribute sts across 3 DPNs, place marker and begin working in rounds.

RND 1: Kfb 6 times. (12 sts)
RND 2: (Kfb, K1) 6 times. (18 sts)
RND 3: (Kfb, K2) 6 times. (24 sts)
RND 4: (Kfb, K3) 6 times. (30 sts)
RND 5: (Kfb, K4) 6 times. (36 sts)
RND 6: (Kfb, K5) 6 times. (42 sts)
RND 7: (Kfb, K6) 6 times. (48 sts)
RND 8: (Kfb, K7) 6 times. (54 sts)
RND 9: (Kfb, K8) 6 times. (60 sts)
RND 10-26: Knit 17 rnds.
RND 27: (K2tog, K8) 6 times. (54 sts)
RND 28: (K2tog, K7) 6 times. (48 sts)
RND29: (K2tog, K6) 6 times. (42 sts)
RND 30: (K2tog, K5) 6 times. (36 sts)
RND 31: (K2tog, K4) 6 times. (30 sts)
RND 32: (K2tog, K3) 6 times. (24 sts)

Continue to work decrease rounds, adding stuffing as you go.

RND 33: (K2tog, K2) 6 times. (18 sts)
RND 34: (K2tog, K1) 6 times. (12 sts)

RND 35: K2tog 6 times. (6 sts)

Cut yarn and thread through remaining 6 sts (adding more stuffing if required), pull to tighten and secure.

Weave in ends.

EARS (make 2)

With cream yarn (color 03), two threads held together, and using US 4 (3.5mm) needles, make a closed magic ring of 6 sts.

Distribute sts across 3 DPNs, place marker and begin working in rounds.

RND 1: Kfb 6 times. (12 sts)
RND 2: (Kfb, K1) 6 times. (18 sts)
RND 3: (Kfb, K2) 6 times. (24 sts)
RND 4: (Kfb, K3) 6 times. (30 sts)
RND 5: (Kfb, K4) 6 times. (36 sts)
RND 6: (K2tog, YO) 18 times. (36 sts)
RND 7: Knit.
RND 8: (K2tog, K4) 6 times. (30 sts)
RND 9: (K2tog, K3) 6 times. (24 sts)
RND 10: (K2tog, K2) 6 times. (18 sts)
RND 11: (K2tog, K1) 6 times. (12 sts)
RND 12: K2tog 6 times. (6 sts)

Do not stuff.

Cut yarn and thread through remaining 6 sts, pull to tighten and secure.

Weave in ends.

HAT

With brown yarn (color 116), two threads held together, and using US 6 (4mm) needles CO 60 sts

Distribute sts across 3 DPNs, place marker and join to work in rounds, being careful not to twist cast on edge.

RND 1-7: K2, P2 (15 times).

Change to light blue yarn (color 071).

RND 8-15: Knit 8 rnds.
RND 16: K20, bind off 8 sts, K8, bind off 8 sts, K14. (44 sts)

Change to brown yarn (color 116).

RND 17: K20, CO 8 sts, K9, CO 8 sts, K15. (60 sts)
RND 18-19: Knit 2 rnds.

Change to cream yarn, (color 03).
RND 20: (K2tog, K8) 6 times. (54 sts)

RND 21: Knit.

Change to brown yarn (color 116).
RND 22: Knit.

Change to light blue yarn (color 071).
RND 23: (K2tog, K7) 6 times. (48 sts)
RND 24: (K2tog, K6) 6 times. (42 sts)
RND 25: (K2tog, K5) 6 times. (36 sts)
RND 26: (K2tog, K4) 6 times. (30 sts)
RND 27: (K2tog, K3) 6 times. (24 sts)
RND 28: (K2tog, K2) 6 times. (18 sts)

Change to brown yarn (color 116).
RND 29: (K2tog, K1) 6 times. (12 sts)
RND 30: K2tog 6 times. (6 sts)

Cut yarn and thread through remaining 6 sts, pull to tighten and secure.

Weave in ends.

SCARF
With cream yarn (color 03), two threads held together, and using US 6 (4mm) needles CO 7 sts.

Knitted flat.

Row 1-10: Knit 10 rows.

Change to brown yarn (color 116).
Row 11-16: Knit 6 rows.

Change to cream yarn (color 03).
Row 17-26: Knit 10 rows.

Change to light blue yarn (color 071).
Row 27-56: Knit 30 rows.
Rows 57-168: Repeat Rows 1-56 twice more.

Change to cream yarn (color 03).
Row 169-194: Repeat Rows 1-26 once more.

Bind off.

ASSEMBLING AND FINISHING
1. Knit all the parts.
2. Sew the head onto the body.
3. Position the hat onto the head.
4. Place the ears into the holes of the hat and secure them with pins.
5. Sew ears to the head.
6. Sew the glass eyes to the head.
7. Glue the plastic nose into place.
8. Apply pink blush to cheeks.
9. Dress with the scarf.

Intelligent Snail

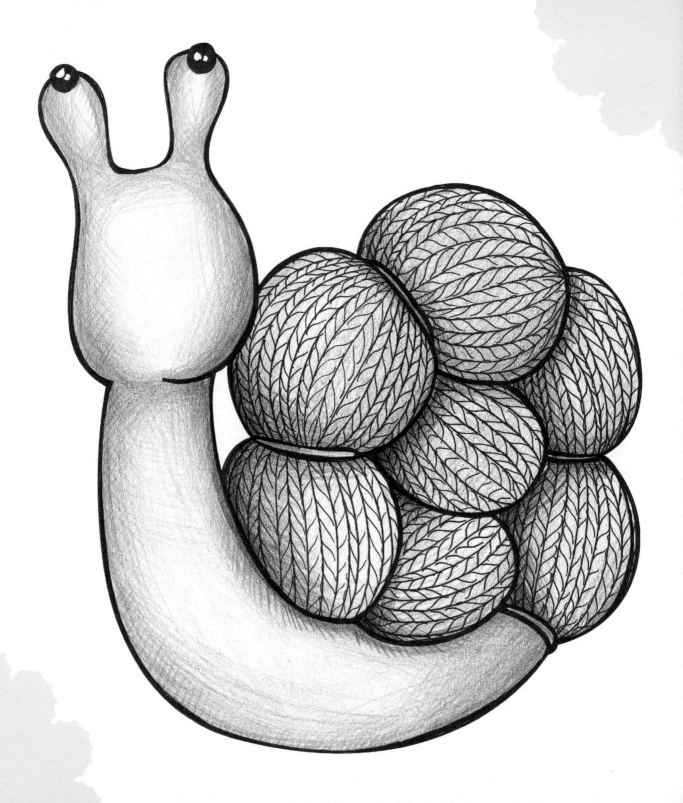

88

ABBREVIATIONS

CO cast on
DPN(s) double pointed needle(s)
K knit
K2tog knit 2 together
Kfb knit into front and back of stitch
P purl
RND round
sl slip purlwise
st(s) stitch(es)

MATERIALS NEEDED

• US 2½ (3mm) 4 double-pointed needles.
• Crochet hook of similar size to needles
• **DMC Woolly yarn 50g/125m**
Colors: 1 ball each of blue (071) and beige (110)
• **DMC Natura Just Cotton 50g/155m**
Color: 1 ball of pink
        (Erica N51)
• Toy Stuffing
• Tapestry needle
• Stitch marker
• 1 pair of black beads for snail's eyes (4 mm)
• 2 safety pins
• Flexible aluminum wire (2 mm)
• Masking tape

NOTES

Finished toy is approximately 6.6" (17 cm) tall.

Gauge (tension) is not critical, but when knitting toys the knitted fabric should be worked fairly tightly to ensure a dense fabric that will hold the stuffing in. If you are a loose knitter you may wish to use smaller needles than size stated.

See page 22 for how to make magic rings.

BODY

Head and eyes are knitted in one piece.

Using blue yarn (color 071), make an open magic ring of 6 sts.

Distribute sts across 3 DPNs, place marker and begin working in rounds.

RND 1: Kfb 6 times. (12 sts)
RND 2: (Kfb, K1) 6 times. (18 sts)
RND 3: (Kfb, K2) 6 times. (24 sts)
RND 4: (Kfb, K3) 6 times. (30 sts)
RND 5: (Kfb, K4) 6 times. (36 sts)
RND 6-18: Knit 13 rnds.

Change to pink yarn (color N51).
RND 19-20: Knit 2 rnds.

Change to blue yarn (color 071).
RND 21-35: Knit 15 rnds.

Change to pink yarn (color N51).
RND 36-37: Knit 2 rnds.

Change to blue yarn (color 071).
RND 38: (K2tog, K10) 3 times. (33 sts)

RND 39-51: Knit 13 rnds.

Change to pink yarn (color N51).
RND 52-53: Knit 2 rnds.

Change to blue yarn (color 071).
RND 54-67: Knit 14 rnds.

Change to pink yarn (color N51).
RND 68-69: Knit 2 rnds.

Change to blue yarn (color 071).
RND 70: (K2tog, K9) 3 times. (30 sts)

RND 71-83: Knit 13 rnds.

Change to pink yarn (color N51).
RND 84-85: Knit 2 rnds.

Change to blue yarn (color 071).
RND 86-99: Knit 14 rnds.

Change to pink yarn (color N51).
RND 100-101: Knit 2 rnds.

Change to blue yarn (color 071).
RND 102: (K2tog, K8) 3 times. (27 sts)

Continue to work decrease rounds, adding stuffing as you go, but don't stuff the body tightly.

RND 103-117: Knit 15 rnds.

Shape neck

Change to beige yarn (color 110).
RND 118: (K2tog, K7) 3 times. (24 sts)
RND 119-150: Knit 32 rnds.
RND 151: (K2tog, K2) 6 times. (18 sts)
RND 152-165: Knit 13 rnds.
RND 166: (K2tog, K4) 3 times. (15 sts)
RND 167-175: Knit 9 rnds.

Shape head

RND 176: (Kfb, K4) 3 times. (18 sts)
RND 177: Knit.
RND 178: (Kfb, K5) 3 times. (21 sts)
RND 179: Knit.
RND 180: (Kfb, K6) 3 times. (24 sts)
RND 181-190: Knit 10 rnds.

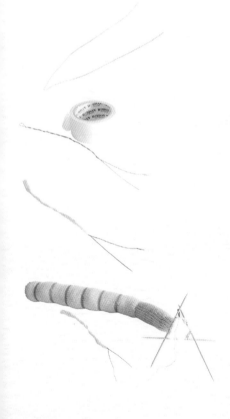

Take a piece of aluminium armature wire 50 cm long. Bend it in the middle and twist the ends around each other. Leave the ends (about 7 cm) untwisted. Secure the twisted part of wire by wrapping well with masking tape. Put this armature inside the snail so the wrapped end

of armature in line with where yarn changes form blue to beige. Ensure the unwrapped ends of wire are protruding to outside.

Shape holes for eyes.

RND 191: sl5, K7, sl5, K7. (14 sts)
RND 192: sl 5 sts onto a safety pin, K7, sl 5 sts onto second safety pin, K7. (14 sts)

Pull the ends of the wire through the holes for eyes.

Stuff the neck and the head tightly.

RND 193: (K2tog, K5) twice. (12 sts)
RND 194: K2tog 6times. (6 sts)

Cut yarn and thread through remaining 6 sts (adding more stuffing if required). Pull to tighten and secure.

Weave in ends.

KNITTING EYES (make 2)
Sl 5 sts back from safety pin onto 2 DPNs. With a third DPN pick up and knit 2 sts around the perimeter of the hole. You now have 7 sts on 3 needles. Keeping wire inside the knitting, place marker and join to work in the round.

RND 1: K2tog, K2, K2tog, K1. (5 sts)
RND 2-6: Knit 5 rnds.
RND 7: Kfb 5times. (10 sts)
RND 8-10: Knit 3 rnds.
RND 11: K2tog 5times. (5 sts)

Bend end of wire and twist to form a loop. Wrap well with masking tape.

Ensuring wire is inside of the eye, cut yarn and thread through remaining 5sts (adding more stuffing if required).

Weave in ends.

Complete second eye to match.

ASSEMBLING AND FINISHING
1. Knit the snail with wire armature inside.
2. Make 7 segments: tightly wrap blue yarn around pink stripes of snail's body, knot to secure and hide the ends.
3. Roll the body into a spiral to form shell and sew in place.
4- Sew the beads for eyes.

Sweet
Pink Doll

ABBREVIATIONS

CO cast on
DPN(s) double pointed needle(s)
K knit
K2tog knit 2 together
K3tog knit 3 together
Kfb knit into front and back of stitch
P purl
RND round
sl1 wyif with yarn in front, slip 1 st purlwise.
st(s) stitch(es)
YO yarn over

MATERIALS NEEDED

• US 2½ (3mm) 4 double-pointed needles.
• Crochet hook of similar size to needles
• **DMC Woolly yarns 50g/125m**
Colors: 1 ball of
        cream (110)
        violet (065)
2 balls of
        pink (042)
• Toy Stuffing
• Tapestry needle
• Stitch marker
• White lace
• sewing thread to match lace
• Pink blush

NOTES

Finished doll is approximately 9.4" (24 cm) tall.

Gauge (tension) is not critical, but when knitting toys the knitted fabric should be worked fairly tightly to ensure a dense fabric that will hold the stuffing in. If you are a loose knitter you may wish to use smaller needles than size stated.

See page 22 for how to make magic rings.

See page 26 for how to work in double knitting.

BODY

Body is made using the double knitting technique.

Using pink yarn (color 042) CO 64 sts.

Row 1-8: (K1, sl1 wyif) to end. (64 sts)
Row 9: K3tog, sl1 wyif (K1, sl1 wyif) to last 4 sts, K1, K3tog. (60 sts)
Row 10: (K1, sl1 wyif) to end.
Row 11- 24: Repeat Rows 9-10 seven times more. (32 sts)
Row 25-26: (K1, sl1 wyif) to end.
Row 27: K3tog, sl1 wyif, (K1, sl1 wyif)

to last 4 sts, K1, K3tog. (28 sts)
Row 28-30: (K1, sl1 wyif) to end.

Remove all stitches from the needles. Separate the two layers and distribute across 3DPNs, place marker and begin working in the round.

Change to violet yarn (color 065).
RND31: Kfb 28 times. (56 sts)
RND32: (Kfb, K1) 28 times. (84 sts)
RND33: (Kfb, 2K) 28 times. (112 sts)

Change pink yarn (color 042)
RND 34-35: Knit 2 rnds.
RND 36: (Kfb, K55) twice. (114 sts)
RND 37: (YO, K2tog, K1) 3 times.
RND 38: Knit.
RND 39-56: Repeat RND37-38 nine times more. (114 sts)

Bind off.

HEAD

Using cream yarn (color 110) with two threads held together make a closed magic ring of 6 sts.

Distribute sts across 3 DPNs, place marker and begin working in rounds.

RND 1: Kfb 6 times. (12 sts)
RND 2: (Kfb, K1) 6 times. (18 sts)
RND 3: (Kfb, K2) 6 times. (24 sts)

RND 4: (Kfb, K3) 6 times. (30 sts)
RND 5: (Kfb, K4) 6 times. (36 sts)
RND 6: (Kfb, K5) 6 times. (42 sts)
RND 7-17: Knit 11 rnds.
RND 18: (K2tog, K5) 6 times. (36 sts)
RND 19: (K2tog, K4) 6 times. (30 sts)
RND20: (K2tog, K3) 6 times. (24 sts)

Continue to work decrease rounds, adding stuffing as you go.

RND 21: (K2tog, K2) 6 times. (18 sts)
RND 22: (K2tog, K1) 6 times. (12 sts)
RND 23: K2tog 6 times. (6 sts)

Cut yarn and thread through remaining 6 sts (adding more stuffing if required), pull to tighten and secure.

Weave in ends.

LEGS (make 2)
Legs are made using the double

knitting technique.

Using pink yarn (color 042) CO 12 sts.
Row 1-76: (K1, sl1 wyif) 6 times.

Remove all stitches from the needles. Separate the two layers and distribute across 3DPNs ready to work in the round.

From this hole fill just the foot part

with toy stuffing.

Place Marker and begin working in the round.

RND 77: K2tog 6 times. (6 sts)

Cut yarn and thread through remaining 6 sts (adding more stuffing if required), pull to tighten and secure.

Weave in ends.

Form foot by taking a length of yarn and wrapping tightly around the ankle, knot firmly to secure and hide the ends inside.

HAT

Hat is made using the double knitting technique.

Using pink yarn (color 042) CO 84 sts.

Row 1-6: (K1, sl1 wyif) to end.
Row 7: K3tog, sl1 wyif (K1, sl1 wyif) to last 4 sts, K1, K3tog. (80 sts)
Row 8: (K1, sl1 wyif) to end.
Row 9-19: Repeat Row 7 eleven times more. (36 sts)
Row 20-22: (K1, sl1 wyif) to end.

Remove all stitches from the nee-

dles. Separate the two layers and distribute across 3DPNs, place marker and begin working in the round.

RND 23-28: (K1, P1) to end. (36 sts)

Bind off.

FINISHING HAT
Fill the corners of the hat with stuffing. Form 3 bubbles on each side by taking a length of yarn and wrapping tightly around the knitting as per photo, knot firmly to secure and hide the ends inside.

ASSEMBLING AND FINISHING
1. Knit all the parts.
2. Fill the hands part with toy stuffing. Form hands by taking a length of yarn and wrapping tightly around the wrist, knot firmly to secure and hide the ends inside.

3. Slightly fill upper part of the body with toy stuffing.
4. Pin the legs to the waistline from the inside of the toy and secure with running stitch at the outer side of the waist line.
5. Sew the head onto the body.
6. Using sewing thread, decorate hat and body with white lace.
7. Position the hat.
8. Apply pink blush to cheeks.

Marble Doll With Hare

ABBREVIATIONS

Beg begin
CO cast on
K knit
K2tog knit 2 together
Kfb knit into front and back of stitch
P purl
P2tog purl 2 together
RND round
st st stockinette stitch (knit all odd numbered rows, purl all even numbered rows)
st(s) stitch(es)
YO yarn over

MATERIALS NEEDED

• US 2½ (3mm) 4 double-pointed needles
• Crochet hook of similar size to needles
• DMC Woolly yarn 50g/125m
Colors: 2 balls of
              white (01)
3 balls of
              cream (03)
1 ball each of
              pink (042)
              violet (065)
              green (081)
• Toy Stuffing
• Tapestry needle
• Stitch marker
• 1 Pair of black buttons for doll's eyes (10mm)
• 1 Pair of black beads for hare's eyes (2mm)
• Small piece of Brown felt for hare's nose
• 1 pair cotter pins (length – 1½in (40 mm), thickness – 3/32 in (3mm)
• 1 disc (15mm)
• 1 disc (40mm)
• Needle nose pliers
• 4 wooden beads (20 mm)
• Lace ribbon
• Glue
• Pink blush
• Threads for embroidery and stitching lace

NOTES

Finished doll is approximately 20" (51 cm) tall.

Finished hare is approximately 5½in (14 cm) tall.

Gauge (tension) is not critical, but when knitting toys the knitted fabric should be worked fairly tightly to ensure a dense fabric that will hold the stuffing in. If you are a loose knitter you may wish to use smaller needles than size stated.

See page 22 for how to make magic rings.

See page 24 for how to knit I-cord

HEAD

Using cream yarn (color 03) with two threads held together make a closed magic ring of 6 sts.

Distribute sts across 3 DPNs, place marker and begin working in rounds.

RND 1: Kfb 6 times. (12 sts)
RND 2: (Kfb, K1) 6 times. (18 sts)
RND 3: (Kfb, K2) 6 times. (24 sts)
RND 4: (Kfb, K3) 6 times. (30 sts)
RND 5: (Kfb, K4) 6 times. (36 sts)
RND 6: (Kfb, K5) 6 times. (42 sts)
RND 7: (Kfb, K6) 6 times. (48 sts)
RND 8: (Kfb, K7) 6 times. (54 sts)
RND 9-26: Knit 18 rnds.
RND 27: (K2tog, K7) 6 times. (48 sts)
RND 28: (K2tog, K6) 6 times. (42 sts)
RND 29: (K2tog, K5) 6 times. (36 sts)
RND30: (K2tog, K4) 6 times. (30 sts)
RND 31: (K2tog, K3) 6 times. (24 sts)

Continue to work decrease rounds, adding stuffing as you go.

RND 32: (K2tog, K2) 6 times. (18 sts)
RND 33: (K2tog, K1) 6 times. (12 sts)

Making neck joint

Start by inserting one of the legs of one of the cotter pins through the eye of the other cotter pin.

Place the larger disc on one of the cotter pin and using needle nose pliers, bend the ends back tightly over the disc to secure.

Holding by the long part of the pin, insert the disc into head. Cut yarn and thread through remaining 12 sts (adding more stuffing if required). Pull to tighten and secure ensuring the straight pin is protruding out of the neck.

BODY

Using cream yarn (color 03) with two threads held together make an open magic ring of 6 sts.

Distribute sts across 3 DPNs, place marker and begin working in rounds.

RND 1: Kfb 6 times. (12 sts)
RND 2-4: Knit 3 rnds.

Attach head to neck by passing cotter pin into body and through smaller disc. Using needle nose piles bend the ends of cotter pin ends back tightly over the disc to secure.

RND 5: (Kfb, K3) 3 times. (15 sts)
RND 6-7: Knit 2 rnds.
RND 8: (Kfb, K4) 3 times. (18 sts)
RND 9-10: Knit 2 rnds.
RND 11: (Kfb, K5) 3 times. (21 sts)
RND 12-13: Knit 2 rnds.
RND 14: (Kfb, K6) 3 times. (24 sts)
RND1 5-16: Knit 2 rnds.
RND 17: (Kfb, K3) 6 times. (30 sts)
RND 18-34: Knit 17 rnds.
RND 35: (Kfb, K9) 3 times. (33 sts)
RND 36-46: Knit 11 rnds.
RND 47: (Kfb, K10) 3 times. (36 sts)

RND 48-57: Knit 10 rnds.

STUFF THE BODY

RND 58: Purl.
RND 59: Knit.

Work decrease rounds, adding stuffing as you go.

RND 60: (K2tog, K4) 6 times. (30 sts)
RND 61: Knit.
RND 62: (K2tog, K3) 6 times. (24 sts)
RND 63: Knit.
RND 64: (K2tog, K2) 6 times. (18 sts)
RND 65: Knit.
RND 66: (K2tog, K1) 6 times. (12 sts)
RND 67: K2tog 6 times. (6 sts)

Cut yarn and thread through remaining 6 sts (adding more stuffing if required), pull to tighten and secure.

Weave in ends.

UPPER ARMS (make 2)

Using cream yarn (color 03) with two threads held together make a closed magic ring of 6 sts.

Distribute sts across 3 DPNs, place marker and begin working in rounds.

RND 1: (Kfb, K1) 3times. (9 sts)
RND 2-11: Knit 10 rnds.
RND 12: K2tog, K7. (8 sts)
RND 13-22: Knit 10 rnds.
RND 23: K2tog, K6. (7 sts)
RND 24-28: Knit 5 rnds.

Add stuffing.
Cut yarn and thread through remaining 7sts (adding more stuffing if required), pull to tighten and secure.

Weave in ends.

LOWER ARMS (make 2)

Using cream yarn (color 03) with two threads held together make a closed magic ring of 6 sts.

Distribute sts across 3 DPNs, place marker and begin working in rounds.

RND 1: (Kfb, K1) 3times. (9 sts)
RND 2-23: Knit 22 rnds.
RND 24: (K2tog, K1) 3 times. (6 sts)

Add stuffing.

Cut yarn and thread through remaining 6 sts (adding more stuffing if required), pull to tighten and secure.

Weave in ends.

UPPER LEGS (make 2)

Using cream yarn (color 03) with two threads held together make a closed magic ring of 7 sts.

Distribute sts across 3 DPNs, place marker and begin working in rounds.

RND 1: Kfb 7 times. (14 sts)
RND 2-33: Knit 32 rnds.
RND 34: K2tog 7 times. (7 sts)

Add stuffing.
Cut yarn and thread through remaining 6 sts (adding more stuffing if required), pull to tighten and secure.

Weave in ends.

LOWER LEGS (make 2)

Using cream yarn (color 03) with two threads held together make a closed magic ring of 6 sts.

Distribute sts across 3 DPNs, place marker and begin working in rounds.

RND 1: Kfb 6 times. (12 sts)
RND 2: Kfb, K11. (13 sts)
RND 3-11: Knit 9 rnds.

Work decrease rounds, adding stuffing as you go

RND 12: K2tog, K11. (12 sts)
RND 13-22: Knit 10 rnds.
RND 23: K2tog, K10. (11 sts)
RND 24-33: Knit 10 rnds.
RND 34: K2tog, K9. (10 sts)
RND 35-42: Knit 8 rnds.
RND 43: K2tog 5 times. (5 sts)

Add stuffing.
Cut yarn and thread through remaining 6 sts (adding more stuffing if required), pull to tighten and secure.

Weave in ends.

HAIR

Using pink yarn (color 042) with two threads held together make a closed magic ring of 6 sts.

Distribute sts across 3 DPNs, place marker and begin working in rounds.

RND 1: Kfb 6 times. (12 sts)
RND 2: (Kfb, K1) 6 times. (18 sts)
RND 3: (Kfb, K2) 6 times. (24 sts)
RND 4: (Kfb, K3) 6 times. (30 sts)
RND 5: (Kfb, K4) 6 times. (36 sts)
RND 6: (Kfb, K5) 6 times. (42 sts)
RND 7: (Kfb, K6) 6 times. (48 sts)
RND 8: (Kfb, K7) 6 times. (54 sts)
RND 9: (Kfb, K17) 3 times. (57 sts)
RND 10-13: Knit 4 rnds.

Shape bangs

Begin working flat.

Turn work to the wrong side.

Row 14: P1, K1, P to last 2 sts, K1, P1.
Row 15: K1, P1, K2tog, K to last 4 sts, K2tog, P1, K1. (55 sts)
Row 16-17: As Row16-17. (53 sts)
Row 18: P1, K1, P 49, K1, P1.
Row 19: K1, P1, K 49, P1, K1.
Row 20-21: As Row18-19.
Row 22: K4, P35, K14.
Row 23: Bind off 14 sts, P1, K33, P4. (39 sts)
Row 24: Bind off 3sts, K1, P32, K1, P1. (36 sts)
Row 25: K1, P1, K32, P1, K1.
Row 26: P1, K1, P32, K1, P1.
Row 27-28: As Row27-28.
Row 29: K1, P1, K2, K2tog, (K4, K2tog) 4 times, K2, K2tog, P1, K1. (30 sts)
Row 30: P1, K1, P26, K1, P1.

Row 31: K1, P1, K1, K2tog, (K3, K2tog) 4 times, K1, K2tog, P1, K1. (24 sts)
Row 32: P1, K1, P20, K1, P1.
Row 33: K1, P1, K2tog, (K2, K2tog) 4 times, K2tog, P1, K1. (18 sts)
Row 34: P1, K1, P14, K1, P1.
Row 35: K1, P1, K14, P1, K1.
Row 36: As Row34.
Row 37: K1, P1, K1, (K1, K2tog) 4 times, K1, P1, K1. (14 sts)

Bind off.

BIG BUBBLES (make 2)
Using white yarn (color 01) with two threads held together make a closed magic ring of 6 sts.

Distribute sts across 3 DPNs, place marker and begin working in rounds.

RND 1: Kfb 6 times. (12 sts)
RND 2: (Kfb, K1) 6 times. (18 sts)
RND 3: (Kfb, K2) 6 times. (24 sts)
RND 4: (Kfb, K3) 6 times. (30 sts)

Change pink yarn (color 042).
RND 5: (P2, K3) 6 times.
RND 6-16: Work 11 rounds as RND5.

Change white yarn (color 01).

RND 17-18: Work 2 rnds as RND5.
RND 19: (P2, K1, K2tog) 6 times. (24 sts)

Continue to work decrease rounds, adding stuffing as you go.

RND 20: (P2tog, K2tog) 6 times. (12 sts)
RND 21: K2tog 6 times. (6 sts)

Cut yarn and thread through remaining 6 sts (adding more stuffing

if required), pull to tighten and secure.

Weave in ends.

SMALL BUBBLES (make 2)
Using white yarn (color 01) with two threads held together make a closed magic ring of 6 sts.

Distribute sts across 3 DPNs, place marker and begin working in rounds.

RND 1: Kfb 6 times. (12 sts)
RND 2: (Kfb, K1) 6 times. (18 sts)
RND 3-9: Knit 7 rnds.

Work decrease rounds, adding stuffing as you go.

RND 10: (K2tog, K1) 6 times. (12 sts)
RND 11: K2tog 6 times. (6 sts)

Cut yarn and thread through remaining 6 sts (adding more stuffing if required), pull to tighten and secure.

Weave in ends.

DRESS

Using violet yarn (color 065) CO 26 sts.

Knitted flat.

Row 1: Knit.
Row 2: (K4, YO, K1, YO) twice, K6, (YO, K1, YO, K4) twice. (34 sts)
Row 3: K2, P30, K2. (34 sts)
Row 4: K5, YO, K1, YO, K6, YO, K1, YO, K8, YO, K1, YO, K6, YO, K1, YO, K5. (42 sts)
Row 5: K2, P38, K2. (34 sts)
Row 6: K6, YO, K1, YO, K8, YO, K1, YO, K10, YO, K1, YO, K8, YO, K1, YO, K6. (50 sts)
Row 7: K2, P46, K2. (50 sts)

Shaping sleeves
Row 8: K8, bind off 9sts, K14, bind off 9sts, K8. (32 sts)

(We now have 8 sts – 15 sts – 9 sts on the needle)

Change to white yarn (color 01).
Row 9: K2, P7, CO 5sts, K15, CO 5sts, P6, K2. (42 sts)
Row 10: K14, (Kfb, K1) 7 times, K14. (49 sts)
Row 11: K2, P 45, K2.
Row 12: Knit.
Row 13-22: Rep Row11-12 à further 5 times.

Distribute sts across 3 DPNs, place marker and begin working in rounds.

RND 23-24: Knit 2 rnds.
RND 25: (K6, Kfb) 7 times. (56 sts)
RND 26-36: Knit 11 rnds.

Change to green yarn, (color 081).
RND 37-38: Knit 2 rnds.

Change to violet yarn (color 065).
RND 39: (Kfb, K1) 28 times). (84 sts)
RND 40-42: Knit 3 rnds.
RND 43: (Kfb, K2) 28 times. (112 sts)
RND 44-58: Knit 15 rows.

Bind off.

STOCKINGS (make 2)
Using violet yarn (color 065) CO 14 sts

Distribute sts across 3 DPNs. Place marker and join for working in the round, being careful not to twist cast on edge.

RND 1-6: Knit 6 rnds.

Change to green yarn, (color 081).
RND 7-8: Knit 2 rnds.

Change to violet yarn (color 065).
RND 9-10: Knit 2 rnds.
RND 7-10 form green and violet stripe pattern
RND 11-22: Rep RND7-10 a further 3 times.
Continue with violet yarn (color 065) only.
RND 23: Knit.
RND 24: K2tog, K5 twice. (12 sts)
RND 25-33: Knit 9 rnds.
RND 34: K2tog 6 times. (6 sts)

Cut yarn and thread through remaining 6 sts, pull to tighten and secure.

Weave in ends.

Using sewing thread in a color to match, take a length of lace and stitch it to the edge of stockings.

ASSEMBLING AND FINISHING
1. Make all the parts.
2. Finish arms: Take both parts of arm (upper and lower) and one bead. Sew the bead to join them together.
3. Finish legs in the same manner.
4. Sew the arms to the body.
5. Sew legs to the bottom of the body.
6. Sew on buttons for eyes.
7. Position the hair to the head and secure with pins. Sew in place.
8. Sew each small bubble onto a big bubble and then sew in place on either side of the hair.
9. Apply pink blush to cheeks.
10. Decorate dress and stockings: Using sewing thread in a color to match, take a length of lace and stitch it around hem of dress and to the edge of stockings.
11. Sew a tiny button to the back neck opening as a fastening for the dress.

HARE

BODY

The body and the head are knitted in one piece.

Using green yarn (color 081) with two threads held together make a closed magic ring of 6 sts.

Distribute sts across 3 DPNs, place marker and begin working in rounds.

RND 1: (Kfb, K1) 3 times. (9 sts)
RND 2: (Kfb, K2) 3 times. (12 sts)
RND 3-11: Knit 9 rnds.

Work decrease rounds, adding stuffing as you go

RND 12: (K2tog, K2) 3 times. (9 sts)
RND 13: (K2tog, K1) 3 times. (6 sts)
RND 14: (Kfb, K1) 3 times. (9 sts)
RND 15-16: Knit 2 rnds.
RND 17: (Kfb, K2) 3 times. (12 sts)
RND 18: Knit.

Change to white yarn (color 01).
RND 19: Knit.
RND 20: (Kfb, K3) 3 times. (15 sts)
RND 21-22: Knit 2 rnds.
RND 23: (Kfb, K4) 3 times. (18 sts)
RND 24: Knit.
RND 25: (Kfb, K2) 6 times. (24 sts)

Change to green yarn (color 081).
RND26: Knit.

Continue to work decrease rounds, adding stuffing as you go.

RND 27: (K2tog, K2) 6 times. (18 sts)
RND 28: (K2tog, K1) 6 times. (12 sts)
RND 29: K2tog 6 times. (6 sts)

Cut yarn and thread through remaining 6 sts (adding more stuffing if required), pull to tighten and secure.

Weave in ends.

ARMS (make 2)
Using green yarn (color 081) with two threads held together CO 4 sts.

Knit as for i-cord.

RND 1-12: Knit 12 rnds.

RND 13: (Kfb, K1) twice. (6 sts)
RND 14-15: Knit 2 rnds.
RND 16: (K2tog, K1) twice. (4 sts)

Do not stuff.

Cut yarn and thread through remaining 4 sts, pull to tighten and secure.

Weave in ends.

LEGS (make 2)
Using green yarn (color 081) with two threads held together make a closed magic ring of 5 sts.

Distribute sts across 3 DPNs, place marker and begin working in rounds.

RND 1-10: Knit 10 rnds.
RND 11: Kfb, K4. (6 sts)
RND 12-19: Knit 8 rnds.
RND 20: K2tog 3 times. (3 sts)

Place a small amount of stuffing into the foot only, do not stuff the legs.

Cut yarn and thread through remaining 3 sts, pull to tighten and secure.

Weave in ends.

EARS (make 2)
Using green yarn (color 081) with

two threads held together CO 3 sts.

Knitted flat.

Row 1-20: Beg with a knit row work 20 rows in st st.
Row 21: K1, Kfb, K1. (4 sts)
Row 22-28: Beg with a purl row work 7 rows in st st.
Row 29: K1, Kfb, K2. (5 sts)
Row 30-36: Beg with a purl row work 7 rows in st st.
Row 37: K2tog, K1, K2tog. (3 sts)

Bind off.

TAIL
Using green yarn (color 081) with two threads held together CO 3 sts.

Knit as for i-cord.

RND 1: Kfb 3 times. (6 st)
RND 2: Knit.
RND 3: K2tog 3 times. (3 sts)

Cut yarn and thread through remaining 3 sts, pull to tighten and secure.

Weave in ends.

ASSEMBLING AND FINISHING
1. Knit all the parts.
2. Sew the arms and the legs to the body.
3. Pin the ears in place then sew them to the head.
4. Sew the tail to the body.
5. Cut the nose from Brown felt and glue in place to the face.
6. Sew the beads as eyes.
7. Embroider mouth, nose and eyebrows.

Giraffe
Tanoshi Doll

ABBREVIATIONS

CO cast on
DPN(s) double pointed needle(s)
K knit
K2tog knit 2 together
Kfb knit into front and back of stitch
P purl
RND round
sts stitches

MATERIALS NEEDED

• US 6 (4 mm) 4 double-pointed needles.
• Crochet hook of similar size to needles
• **DMC Natura Just Cotton XL yarn 100g/75m**
Colors: 1 ball each of
      white (01)
      black (02)
      yellow (09)
• Toy Stuffing
• Tapestry needle
• Stitch marker
• 1 pair of black buttons (10 mm)
• Pink blush
• Brown colored felt
• Glue

NOTES

Finished doll is approximately 10.2" (26 cm) tall.

Gauge (tension) is not critical, but when knitting toys the knitted fabric should be worked fairly tightly to ensure a dense fabric that will hold the stuffing in. If you are a loose knitter you may wish to use smaller needles than size stated.

See page 22 for how to make open or closed magic ring.

See page 24 for how to knit i-cord.

HEAD

Using white yarn (color 01) make an open magic ring of 6 sts.

Distribute sts across 3 DPNs, place marker and begin working in rounds.

RND 1: Kfb 6 times. (12 sts)
RND 2: (Kfb, K1) 6 times. (18 sts)
RND 3: (Kfb, K2) 6 times. (24 sts)
RND 4: (Kfb, K3) 6 times. (30 sts)
RND 5: (Kfb, K4) 6 times. (36 sts)
RND 6: (Kfb, K5) 6 times. (42 sts)
RND 7: (Kfb, K6) 6 times. (48 sts)
RND 8-21: Knit 14 rnds.
RND 22: (K2tog, K6) 6 times. (42 sts)

RND 23: (K2tog, K5) 6 times. (36 sts)
RND 24: (K2tog, K4) 6 times. (30 sts)
RND 25: (K2tog, K3) 6 times. (24 sts)

Continue to work decrease rounds, adding stuffing as you go.

RND 26: (K2tog, K2) 6 times. (18 sts)
RND 27: (K2tog, K1) 6 times. (12 sts)
RND 28: K2tog 6 times. (6 sts)

Cut yarn and thread through remaining 6 sts (adding more stuffing if required). Pull to tighten and secure, leaving a small hole for sewing the head to the body.

Weave in ends.

BODY

Using white yarn (color 01) make an open magic ring of 6 sts.

Distribute sts across 3 DPNs, place marker and begin working in rounds.

RND 1: Kfb 6 times. (12 sts)
RND 2: (Kfb, K1) 6 times. (18 sts)
RND 3: (Kfb, K7, Kfb) twice. (22 sts)
RND 4: (Kfb, K9, Kfb) twice. (26 sts)

Change to yellow yarn (color 09).
RND 5-7: Purl 3 rnds.
RND 8: Knit.
RND 9: Purl.
RND 10: (K2tog, K9, K2tog) twice. (22 sts)
RND 11-12: Knit 2 rnds.
RND 13: (K2tog, K7, K2tog) twice. (18 sts)
RND 14-15: Knit 2 rnds.
RND 16: (K2tog, K5, K2tog) twice. (14 sts)
RND 17-19: Knit 3 rnds.

Continue to work decrease rounds, adding stuffing as you go.

RND 20: (K2tog, K3, K2tog) twice. (10 sts)
RND 21-32: Knit 12 rnds.
RND 33: K2tog, K8. (9 sts)
RND 34-36: Knit 3 rnds.

Cut yarn and thread through remaining 9 sts (adding more stuffing if required), pull to tighten and secure.

Weave ends.

HOOD

Using yellow yarn (color 09) make a closed magic ring of 6 sts.

Distribute sts across 3 DPNs, place marker and begin working in rounds.

RND 1: Kfb 6 times. (12 sts)
RND 2: (Kfb, K1) 6 times. (18 sts)
RND 3: (Kfb, K2) 6 times. (24 sts)
RND 4: (Kfb, K3) 6 times. (30 sts)
RND 5: (Kfb, K4) 6 times. (36 sts)
RND 6: (Kfb, K5) 6 times. (42 sts)
RND 7: (Kfb, K6) 6 times. (48 sts)
RND 8: (Kfb, K7) 6 times. (54 sts)
RND 9-22: Knit 14 rnds.

Begin working flat.

Turn work to the wrong side.

Row 23: P2tog, P to last 2 sts, P2tog. (52 sts)
Row 24: K2tog, K to last 2 sts, K2tog. (50 sts)
Row 25: K2tog, K15, K2tog, K14, K2tog, K15. (47 sts)
Row 26: Knit.
Row 27: K2tog, K14, K2tog, K13, K2tog, K14. (44 sts)
Row 28: K13, K2tog, K14, K2tog, K13. (42 sts)

Bind off.

ARMS (make 2)
Using white yarn (color 01) CO 3 sts.

Knit as i-cord.

RND 1-13: Knit 13 rnds.

Do not stuff.

Cut yarn and thread through remaining 3 sts, pull to tighten and secure.

Weave in ends.

SLEEVES (make 2)
Using yellow yarn (color 09) make a closed magic ring of 5 sts.

Distribute sts across 3 DPNs, place marker and begin working in rounds.

RND 1-4: Knit 4 rnds
RND 5: Purl.
RND 6: Knit.
RND 5: Purl.

Bind off.

Weave in ends.

EARS (make 2)
Using yellow yarn (color 09) make a closed magic ring of 4 sts.

Distribute sts across 3 DPNs, place marker and begin working in rounds.

RND 1: Kfb 4 times. (8 sts)

RND 2: (Kfb, K2, Kfb) twice. (12 sts)
RND 3-4: Knit 2 rnds.
RND 5: (Kfb, K4, Kfb) twice. (16 sts)
RND 6: Knit.
RND 7: (Kfb, K6, Kfb) twice. (20 sts)
RND 8-9: Knit 2 rnds.
RND 10: (K2tog, K6, K2tog) twice. (16 sts)
RND 11-12: Knit 2 rnds.
RND 13: (K2tog, K4, K2tog) twice. (12 sts)
RND 14-15: Knit 2 rnds.
RND 16: (K2tog, K2, K2tog) twice. (8 sts)
RND 17-18: Knit 2 rnds.
RND 19: K2tog 4 times. (4 sts)

Do not stuff.

Cut yarn and thread through remaining 4 sts, pull to tighten and secure.

Weave in ends

OSSICONES (antlers) (make 2)
Using yellow yarn (color 09) CO 5 sts.

Distribute sts across 3 DPNs, place marker and join for working in the round, being careful not to twist cast on edge.

RND 1-10: Knit 10 rnds.

Change to white yarn (color 01).
RND 11: Kfb 5 times. (10 sts)
RND 12-16: Knit 5 rnds.

Work decrease rounds, adding stuffing as you go.

RND 17: K2tog 5 times. (5 sts)

Cut yarn and thread through remaining 5 sts (adding more stuffing if required), pull to tighten and secure.

Weave in ends.

TAIL
Using yellow yarn (color 09) CO 2 sts

Knit as i-cord.

RND 1-10: Knit 10 rnds.
RND 11: K2tog. (1 st)
RND 12-15: Knit 4 rnds.

Fasten off.

Make tassel from white yarn (color 01) and sew it to the tail.

ASSEMBLING AND FINISHING
1. Knit all the parts.
2. Sew the head onto the body.
3. Insert the arms into the sleeves. I used a crochet hook for this.
4. Sew the arms to the body.
5. Embroider the dolls hair using black yarn (color 02).
6. Position the hood on the head and sew in place along the neck line.
7. Sew on buttons for eyes.
8. Pin the ears and antlers in place then sew them to the hood.
9. Apply pink blush to cheeks.
10. Sew the tail to the body.
11. Cut small pieces from brown felt and glue these to the body and hood.

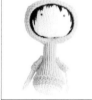

Naptime Doll

ABBREVIATIONS

Beg begin

C4F Cable 4 forward: slip next 4 sts on cable needle and hold at front of work, knit 4, knit the 4 sts from the cable needle.

C5F Cable 5 forward: put next 5 sts on cable needle and hold at front of work, knit 5, knit the 5 sts from the cable needle.

CO cast on

K knit

K2tog knit 2 together

Kfb knit into front and back of stitch

P purl

RND round

st st stockinette stitch (knit all odd numbered rows, purl all even numbered rows)

st(s) stitch(es)

MATERIALS NEEDED

• US 6 (4 mm) 4 double-pointed needles.
• Crochet hook of similar size to needles
• DMC Natura Just Cotton XL yarn 100g/75m
Colors: 1 ball of
        cream (03)
2 balls of
        pink (042)
• Toy Stuffing
• Tapestry needle
• Stitch marker
• Pink blush
• Thread for embroidering eyes

NOTES

Finished doll is approximately 17.3" (44 cm) tall.

Gauge (tension) is not critical, but when knitting toys the knitted fabric should be worked fairly tightly to ensure a dense fabric that will hold the stuffing in. If you are a loose knitter you may wish to use smaller needles than size stated.

See page 22 for how to make magic rings.

See page 24 for how to knit I-cord

BODY

Body and head are the knitted in one piece.

Using cream yarn (color 03) make a closed magic ring of 6 sts.

Distribute sts across 3 DPNs, place marker and begin working in rounds.

RND 1: Kfb 6 times. (12 sts)
RND 2: (Kfb, K1) 6 times. (18 sts)
RND 3: (Kfb, K2) 6 times. (24 sts)
RND 4: (Kfb, K3) 6 times. (30 sts)
RND 5: (Kfb, K4) 6 times. (36 sts)
RND 6: (Kfb, K5) 6 times. (42 sts)
RND 7-19: Knit 13 rnds.
RND 20: (K2tog, K5) 6 times. (36 sts)
RND 21: (K2tog, K4) 6 times. (30 sts)
RND 22: (K2tog, K3) 6 times. (24 sts)

Continue to work decrease rounds, adding stuffing as you go.

RND 23: (K2tog, K2) 6 times. (18 sts)
RND 24: (K2tog, K1) 6 times. (12 sts)

Change to pink yarn (color 042).

RND 25: Kfb 12 times. (24 sts)
RND 26: Knit.
RND 27: K2, P1, K6, P1, K14.
RND 28-30: Work 3 rnds as RND27.
RND 31: K2, P1, Kfb, K4, Kfb, P1, K2, Kfb, K10, Kfb. (28 sts)
RND 32: K2, P1, K8, P1, K16.
RND 33: K2, P1, C4F, P1, K16.
RND 34-35: Work 2 rnds as RND32.
RND 36: Kfb, K1, P1, K8, P1, K1, Kfb twice, K12, Kfb. (32 sts)
RND 37: K3, P1, K8, P1, K19.
RND 38-39: Work 2 rnds as RND37.
RND 40: Kfb, K2, P1, K8, P1, K2, Kfb twice, K14, Kfb. (36 sts)
RND 41: K4, P1, K8, P1, K22.
RND 42: Kfb, K3, P1, C4F, P1, K3, Kfb twice, K16, Kfb. (40 sts)
RND 43: K5, P1, K8, P1, K25.
RND 44-49: Work 6 rnds as RND43.
RND 50: K5, P1, Kfb, K6, Kfb, P1, K5, Kfb, K18, Kfb. (44 sts)
RND 51: K5, P1, K10, P1, K27.
RND 52: As RND51.
RND 53: K5, P1, C5F, P1, K27.
RND 54: K5, P1, K10, P1, K27.
RND 55: Kfb, K4, P1, K10, P1, K4, Kfb twice, K20, Kfb. (48 sts)
RND 56: K6, P1, K10, P1, K30. (48 sts)
RND 57-59: Work 3 rnds as RND56.
RND 60: Kfb, K5, P1, K10, P1, K5, Kfb twice, K22, Kfb. (52 sts)
RND 61: K7, P1, K10, P1, K33.
RND 62: As RND61.
RND 63: K7, P1, C5F, P1, K33.
RND 64: K7, P1, K10, P1, K33.
RND 65-67: Work 3 rnds as RND64.

Bind off.

ARMS (make 2)

Using cream yarn (color 03) make a closed magic ring of 6 sts.

Distribute sts across 3 DPNs, place marker and begin working in rounds.

RND 1: (Kfb, K1) 3 times. (9 sts)
RND 2-25: Knit 24 rnds.
RND 26: (K2tog, K1) 3 times. (6 sts)

Do not stuff.

Cut yarn and thread through remaining 6 sts, pull to tighten and secure.

Weave in ends.

LEGS (make 2)

Using pink yarn (color 042) make a closed magic ring of 5 sts.

Distribute sts across 3 DPNs, place marker and begin working in rounds.

RND 1: Kfb 5 times. (10 sts)
RND 2-9: Knit 8 rnds.

Change to cream yarn (color 03).
RND 10-14: Knit 5 rnds.

Change pink yarn (color 042).
RND 15-19: Knit 5 rnds.
RND 10-19 form cream and pink stripe pattern.
RND 20-39: Rep RND 10-19 twice more.

Continue with cream yarn (color 03) only.

RND 40-48: Knit 9 rnds.

Do not stuff. Bind off.

HAIR

Using pink yarn (color 042) make a closed magic ring of 5 sts.

Distribute sts across 3 DPNs, place marker and begin working in rounds.

RND 1: kfb 6 times. (12 sts)
RND 2: (Kfb, K1) 6 times. (18 sts)
RND 3: (Kfb, K2) 6 times. (24 sts)

RND 4: (Kfb, K3) 6 times. (30 sts)
RND 5: (Kfb, K4) 6 times. (36 sts)
RND 6: (Kfb, K5) 6 times. (42 sts)
RND 7: (Kfb, K13) 3 times. (45 sts)
RND 8-13: Knit 6 rnds.
RND 14: P15, K30. (45 sts)

Shape bangs.

RND 15: Bind off 14sts, K30. (31 sts)

Begin working flat.

Turn work to the wrong side.

Row 16-20: Beg with a purl row work 5 rows in st st.
Row 21: K1, Kfb, K27, Kfb, K1. (33 sts)
Row 22-23: Beg with a purl row work 2 rows in st st.
Row 24: P1, Kfb, P29, Kfb, P1. (35 sts)
Row 25-26: Beg with a knit row work 2 rows in st st.
Row 27-28: Knit 2 rows.

Bind off.

ASSEMBLING AND FINISHING

1. Sew the arms to the body.
2. Position the legs inside of the body and secure with pins.
3. Sew along lower edge of the dress, closing the opening and securing legs.
4. Position the hair onto the head and sew in place.
5. Mark the position for the eyes with pins and then embroider the eyes as shown in the photos.
6. Apply pink blush to cheeks.

Pink Flower Doll

ABBREVIATIONS

CO cast on
DPN(s) double pointed needle(s)
K knit
K2tog knit 2 together
Kfb knit into front and back of stitch
P purl
P2tog purl 2 together
RND round
sl1 wyif with yarn in front, slip 1 st purlwise.
st(s) stitch(es)
YO yarn over

MATERIALS NEEDED

• US 2½ (3mm) 4 double-pointed needles.
• Crochet hook of similar size to needles
• **DMC Woolly yarn 50g/125m**
Colors: 1 ball each of
  cream (03)
  pink (043)
  light blue (071),
  green (082)
  khaki (083)
• Toy Stuffing
• Tapestry needle
• Stitch marker
• 1 pair of black plastic eyes (6mm alf beads)
• Flexible aluminum wire (2 mm)
• Pink felted flower
• Big light blue beads for decorating hood and bag.
• Pink blush

NOTES

Finished doll is approximately 7" (18 cm) tall.

Gauge (tension) is not critical, but when knitting toys the knitted fabric should be worked fairly tightly to ensure a dense fabric that will hold the stuffing in. If you are a loose knitter you may wish to use smaller needles than size stated.

See page 22 for how to make magic rings.

See page 24 for how to knit i-cord.

See page 26 for how to work double knitting.

HEAD

Using cream yarn (color 03) with two threads held together make an open magic ring of 6 sts.

Distribute sts across 3 DPNs, place marker and begin working in rounds.

RND 1: Kfb 6 times. (12 sts)
RND 2: (Kfb, K1) 6 times. (18 sts)
RND 3: (Kfb, K2) 6 times. (24 sts)
RND 4: (Kfb, K3) 6 times. (30 sts)

RND 5: (Kfb, K4) 6 times. (36 sts)
RND 6: (Kfb, K5) 6 times. (42 sts)
RND 7: (Kfb, K6) 6 times. (48 sts)
RND 8-17: Knit 10 rnds.
RND 18: (K2tog, K6) 6 times. (42 sts)
RND 19: (K2tog, K5) 6 times. (36 sts)
RND 20: (K2tog, K4) 6 times. (30 sts)
RND 21: (K2tog, K3) 6 times. (24 sts)

Continue to work decrease rounds, adding stuffing as you go.

RND 22: (K2tog, K2) 6 times. (18 sts)
RND 23: (K2tog, K1) 6 times. (12 sts)
RND 24: K2tog 6 times. (6 sts)

Cut yarn and thread through remaining 6 sts (adding more stuffing if required). Pull to tighten and secure leaving a small hole for sewing the head to the body.

Weave in ends.

BODY

Starting at the bottom of the body and using pink yarn (color 043) with two threads held together, make an open magic ring of 6 sts.

Distribute sts across 3 DPNs, place marker and begin working in rounds.

RND 1: Kfb 6 times. (12 sts)
RND 2: (Kfb, K1) 6 times. (18 sts)
RND 3: (Kfb, K2) 6 times. (24 sts)
RND 4: Purl.
RND 5-7: Knit 3 rnds.
RND 8: (K2tog, K6) 3 times. (21 sts)
RND 9-10: Knit 2 rnds.
RND 11: (K2tog, K5) 3 times. (18 sts)
RND 12: Knit.
RND 13: (K2tog, K4) 3 times. (15 sts)
RND 14-17: Knit 4 rnds.
RND 18: (K2tog, K3) 3 times. (12 sts)

Continue to work decrease rounds, adding stuffing as you go.

RND 19-20: Knit 2 rnds.
RND 21: K2tog 6 times. (6 sts)

Cut yarn and thread through remaining 6 sts (adding more stuffing if required). Pull to tighten and secure leaving a small hole for sewing the head to the body.

Weave in ends.

DRESS RUFFLE
Using pink yarn (color 043) with two threads held together, pick up and knit 24 sts purl bumps from RND4 of the body.

Distribute sts across 3 DPNs, place marker and begin working in rounds.

RND 1: Kfb 24 times. (48 sts)
RND 2: Knit.
RND 3: (K2tog, YO) 24 times. (48 sts)

Bind off.

COAT

Using light blue yarn (color 071) with two threads held together CO 16 sts.

Knitted flat.

Row 1: Knit.
Row 2: K2, P to last 2 sts, K2.
Row 3: K4, Kfb, K to last 5 sts, Kfb, K4. (18 sts)
Row 4-13: Repeat Rows 2-3 a further 5 times. (28 sts)
Row 14: Knit.
Row 15: K4, Kfb, K18, Kfb, K4. (30 sts)

Bind off.

HOOD

Using light blue yarn (color 071) with two threads held together make a closed magic ring of 6 sts.

Distribute sts across 3 DPNs, place marker and begin working in rounds.

RND 1: Kfb 6 times. (12 sts)
RND 2: (Kfb, K1) 6 times. (18 sts)
RND 3: (Kfb, K2) 6 times. (24 sts)
RND 4: (Kfb, K3) 6 times. (30 sts)
RND 5: (Kfb, K4) 6 times. (36 sts)
RND 6: (Kfb, K5) 6 times. (42 sts)
RND 7: (Kfb, K6) 6 times. (48 sts)
RND 8: (Kfb, K7) 6 times. (54 sts)
RND 9: (Kfb, K8) 6 times. (60 sts)
RND 10-19: Knit 10 rnds.
RND 20: (K2tog, K8) 6 times. (54 sts)
RND 21: (K2tog, K7) 6 times. (48 sts)

Begin working flat.

Turn work to the wrong side.

Row 22: Purl.
Row 23: (K2tog, K6) 6 times. (42 sts)
Row 24: Purl.
Row 25: (K2tog, K5) 6 times. (36 sts)
Row 26-27: Knit 2 rows.

Bind off.

ARMS (make 2)

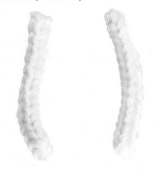

Using cream yarn (color 03) with two threads held together CO 4 sts.

Knit as for i-cord.

RND 1-14: Knit 14 rnds.

Do not stuff.

Cut yarn and thread through remaining 4 sts, pull to tighten and secure.

Weave in ends.

SLEEVES (make 2)

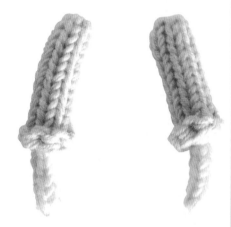

Using light blue yarn (color 071) with two threads held together make a closed magic ring of 7 sts.

Distribute sts across 3 DPNs, place marker and begin working in rounds.

RND 1-11: Knit 11 rnds.
RND 12: Purl.

Bind off.

BAG

Bag is made using the double knitting technique.

Using khaki yarn (color 083) with two threads held together CO 14 sts.

Row 1-12: (1K, Sl1 wyif) 7 times.

Remove all stitches from the needle and separate the two layers between 2 DPNs.

Place marker and begin working in the round.

Change to pink yarn (color 043).
RND 13: Knit.
RND 14: Bind off 7sts, K6. (7 sts)

Begin working flat.

Turn work to the wrong side.

Row 15-16: Knit 2 rows.
Row 17: Purl.
Row 18: Knit.
Row 19: P1, P2tog, P1, P2tog, P1. (5 sts)
Row 20: Knit.
Row 21: P1, bind off 3 sts. (2 sts)
Row 22: K1, CO 3sts, K1. (5 sts)
Bind off.

STRAP OF THE BAG

With pink yarn (color 043) held double CO 2 sts.

Knitted flat.

Row 1-40: Knit 40 rows.

Bind off.

Sew the strap to the bag and sew the big bead as fastener.

SCARF
Using pink yarn (color 043) with two threads held together CO 4 sts.

Knitted flat.

Row 1-6: Knit 6 rows.

Change to khaki yarn (color 083).
Row 7-106: Knit 100 rows.

Change to pink yarn (color 043).
Row 107-112: Knit 6 rows.

Bind off.

ASSEMBLING AND FINISHING

1. Knit all the parts.

2. Sew the head onto the body.

3. Make the hairstyle as shown in tutorial on page 32.

4. Make wire legs as shown in tutorial on page 34.

5. Position the coat on the body and secure it with pins.

6. Insert the arms into the sleeves. I used a crochet hook for this.

7. Sew the arms to the body.

8. Place the hood on the head and sew along the neck line of coat.

9. Make hair braids. Sew them to in place on the head and trim to an even length.

10. Glue the plastic eyes into place.

11. Apply pink blush to cheeks.

12. Sew felted flower to the hood and decorate with bead.

White Bunnies in Hats

ABBREVIATIONS

CO cast on
DPN(s) double pointed needle(s)
K knit
K2tog knit 2 together
K3tog knit 3 together
Kfb knit into front and back of stitch
P purl
RND round
st(s) stitch(es)
YO yarn over

MATERIALS NEEDED

• US 2½ (3mm) 4 double-pointed needles.
• Crochet hook of similar size to needles
• DMC Woolly yarn 50g/125m
Colors: 2 balls of
           white (01)
1 ball each of
           green (084)
           orange (103)
• Toy Stuffing
• Tapestry needle
• Stitch marker
• 2 pair of black beads (4mm)
• 2 plastic noses
• Pompoms
• Glue

NOTLAR

Finished bunnies are approximately 7" (18 cm) tall.

Bunnies are knitted the same except they have different ears and hats.

Gauge (tension) is not critical, but when knitting toys the knitted fabric should be worked fairly tightlyto ensure a dense fabric that willhold the stuffing in. If you are a loose knitter you may wish to use smaller needles than size stated.

See page 22 for how to make magic rings.

See page 24 for how to knit i-cord.

BODY

Body and head are knitted in one piece.

Using white yarn (color 01) with two threads held together make a closed magic ring of 6 sts.

Distribute sts across 3 DPNs, place marker and begin working in rounds.

RND 1: Kfb 6 times. (12 sts)
RND 2: (Kfb, K1) 6 times. (18 sts)
RND 3: (Kfb, K2) 6 times. (24 sts)
RND 4: (Kfb, K3) 6 times. (30 sts)
RND 5: (Kfb, K4) 6 times. (36 sts)
RND 6-20: Knit 15 rnds.
RND 21: K2tog 18 times. (18 sts)
RND 22: (K2tog, K1) 6 times. (12 sts)
RND 23: Kfb 12 times. (24 sts)
RND 24-35: Knit 12 rnds.

Work decrease rounds, adding stuffing as you go.

RND 36: (K2tog, K2) 6 times. (18 sts)

RND 37: (K2tog, K1) 6 times. (12 sts)

RND 38: K2tog 6times. (6 sts)

Cut yarn and thread through remaining 6 sts (adding more stuffingif required), pull to tighten and secure.

Weave in ends.

ARMS (make 2)

Using white yarn (color 01) with two threads held together make a closed magic ring of 6 sts.

Distribute sts across 3 DPNs, place-marker and begin working in rounds.

RND 1-10: Knit 10 rnds.
RND 11: (Kfb, K1) 3 times. (9 sts)
RND 12-14: Knit 3 rnds.

Work decrease rounds, adding stuffing as you go.

RND 15: (K2tog, K1) 3 times. (6 sts)

Cut yarn and thread through remaining 6 sts (adding more stuffing if required), pull to tighten and secure.

Weave in ends.

LEGS (make 2)
Using white yarn (color 01) with two threads held together CO 8 sts.

Distribute sts across 3 DPNs, place marker and join to work in the round, being careful not to twist cast on edge.

RND 1-7: Knit 7 rnds.
RND 8: (Kfb, K1) 4 times. (12 sts)
RND 9-13: Knit 5 rnds.

Work decrease rounds, adding stuffing as you go.

RND 14: (K2tog, K1) 4 times. (8 sts)
RND 15: Knit.
RND 16: K2tog 4 times. (4 sts)

Cut yarn and thread through remaining 4 sts (adding more stuffing if required), pull to tighten and secure.

Weave in ends.

TAIL

Using white yarn (color 01) with two threads held together make a closed magic ring of 4 sts.

Distribute sts across 3 DPNs, place marker and begin working in rounds.

RND 1: Kfb 4 times. (8 sts)
RND 2: (Kfb, K1) 4 times. (12 sts)
RND 3: Knit.

Work decrease rounds, adding stuffing as you go.

RND 4: (K2tog, K1) 4 times. (8 sts)
RND 5: K2tog 4 times. (4 sts)

Cut yarn and thread through remaining 4 sts (adding more stuffing if required), pull to tighten and secure.

Weave in ends.

EARS N1 (make 2)

Using white yarn (color 01) with two threads held together CO 4 sts.

Knitted flat.

Row 1-10: Knit 10 rows.
Row 11: K1, Kfb twice, K1. (6 sts)
Row 12-19: Knit 8 rows.
Row 20: K1, K2tog twice, K1. (4 sts)
Row 21: Knit.
Row 22: K1, K2tog, K1. (3 sts)
Row 21: K3tog. (1 st)

Fasten off.

EARS N2 (make 2)

Using white yarn (color 01) with two threads held together CO 6 sts.

Distribute sts across 3 DPNs, place marker and join to work in the round, being careful not to twist cast on edge.

135

RND 1-2: Knit 2 rnds.
RND 3: (Kfb, K2) twice. (8 sts)
RND 4: Knit.
RND 5: (Kfb, K3) twice. (10 sts)
RND 6-7: Knit 2 rnds.
RND 8: (Kfb, K4) twice. (12 sts)
RND 9-10: Knit 2 rnds.
RND 11: K2tog 6times. (6 sts)

Do not stuff.

Cut yarn and thread through remaining 6 sts, pull to tighten and secure.

Weave in ends.

LIGHT GREEN HAT

Using green yarn (color 084) with one thread only, CO 36 sts.

Knitted flat.

Row 1-2: (K2, P2) 9 times. (36 sts)
Row 3: Knit.
Row 4: Purl.
Row 5: K15, bind off 6 sts, K14. (30sts)
Row 6: P15, CO 6 sts, P15. (36 sts)
Row 7: Knit.
Row 8: Purl.
Row 9: (K2tog, K4) 6 times. (30 sts)

Distribute sts across 3 DPNs, place marker and join to work in the round.

RND 10-11: Knit 2 rnds.
RND 12: (K2tog, K3) 6 times. (24 sts)
RND 13-15: Knit 3 rnds.
RND 16: (K2tog, K2) 6 times. (18 sts)
RND 17: Knit.
RND 18: (K2tog, K1) 6 times. (12 sts)
RND 19: Knit.
RND 20: K2tog 6 times. (6 sts)

Cut yarn and thread through remaining 6 sts, pull to tighten and secure.

Weave in ends.

ORANGE HAT

Using orange yarn (color 103) with one thread only, CO 38 sts.

Knitted flat.

Row 1: (K2, P2) 9 times, K2.
Row 2: (P2, K2) 9 times, P2.
Row 3-4: As Rows 1-2.
Row 5: Knit.
Row 6: Purl.
Row 7: K15, bind off 8 sts, K14. (30sts)

Row 8: P15, CO 8 sts, P15. (38 sts)
Row 9: K1, K2tog, K32, K2tog, K1. (36 sts)
Row 10: Purl.
Row 11: (K2tog, K4) 6 times. (30 sts)

Distribute sts across 3 DPNs, place marker and join to work in the round.

RND 12-14: Knit 3 rnds.
RND 15: (K2tog, K3) 6 times. (24 sts)
RND 16-17: Knit 2 rnds.
RND 18: (K2tog, K2) 6 times. (18 sts)
RND 19: Knit.
RND 20: (K2tog, K1) 6 times. (12 sts)
RND 21: Knit.
RND 22: K2tog 6 times. (6 sts)

Cut yarn and thread through remaining 6 sts, pull to tighten and secure.

Weave in ends.

ASSEMBLING AND FINISHING
1. Knit all the parts.
2. For best shaping of the head and body take a length of yarn and wrap tightly around neck. Pull to tighten and secure with a knot. Snip off the excess yarn.

3. Shaping feet: To make the feet flatter on the base, take a long piece of yarn, and thread it on your needle and knot it on one end. Starting at the underside of the sole, push your needle out through the top of the foot. Taking a small stitch, go back through the foot to the outside of sole. Repeat this process one or two more times, gently pulling the thread to tighten the foot with each pass and being careful not to indent too deeply. Secure thread and snip off the excess yarn.

4. Pin the legs on position and sew them to body.

5. Sew the arms to the body.

6. Sew the tail to the back of the body.

7. Sew on beads for eyes.

8. Position the hat on the head.

9. Place the ears into the hole of the hat and secure them with pins.

10. Sew ears to the head.

11. Glue nose to the head.

12. Make straps with pompoms and sew them to hats.

Dog Tanoshi Doll

ABBREVIATIONS

CO cast on
DPN(s) double pointed needle(s)
K knit
K2tog knit 2 together
Kfb knit into front and back of stitch
P purl
P2tog purl 2 together
RND round
sts stitches

MATERIALS NEEDED

• US 6 (4 mm) 4 double-pointed needles.
• Crochet hook of similar size to needles
• **DMC Natura Just Cotton XL yarn 100g/75m**
Colors: 1 ball each of
    sand (31)
    navy (71)
    cream (91)
    brown (111)
• Toy Stuffing
• Tapestry needle
• Stitch marker
• 1 pair of black buttons (10 mm)
• Pink blush
• Brown colored felt
• Glue

NOTES

Finished doll is approximately 5.9" (15 cm) tall.

Gauge (tension) is not critical, but when knitting toys the knitted fabric should be worked fairly tightly to ensure a dense fabric that will hold the stuffing in. If you are a loose knitter you may wish to use smaller needles than size stated.

See page 22 for how to make open or closed magic ring.

See page 24 for how to knit i-cord.

HEAD
Using cream yarn (color 91) make an open magic ring of 6 sts.

Distribute sts across 3 DPNs, place marker and begin working in rounds.

RND 1: Kfb 6 times. (12 sts)
RND 2: (Kfb, K1) 6 times. (18 sts)
RND 3: (Kfb, K2) 6 times. (24 sts)
RND 4: (Kfb, K3) 6 times. (30 sts)
RND 5: (Kfb, K4) 6 times. (36 sts)
RND 6: (Kfb, K5) 6 times. (42 sts)
RND 7: (Kfb, K6) 6 times. (48 sts)
RND 8-21: Knit 14 rnds.
RND 22: (K2tog, K6) 6 times. (42 sts)
RND 23: (K2tog, K5) 6 times. (36 sts)
RND 24: (K2tog, K4) 6 times. (30 sts)
RND 25: (K2tog, K3) 6 times. (24 sts)

Continue to work decrease rounds, adding stuffing as you go.

RND 26: (K2tog, K2) 6 times. (18 sts)
RND 27: (K2tog, K1) 6 times. (12 sts)
RND 28: K2tog 6 times. (6 sts)

Cut yarn and thread through remaining 6 sts (adding more stuffing if required). Pull to tighten and secure, leaving a small hole for sewing the head to the body.

Weave in ends.

BODY
Using brown yarn (color 111) make an open magic ring of 6 sts.

Distribute sts across 3 DPNs, place marker and begin working in rounds.

RND 1: Kfb 6 times. (12 sts)
RND 2: (Kfb, K1) 6 times. (18 sts)
RND 3: (Kfb, K7, Kfb) twice. (22 sts)

Change sand yarn (color 31).
RND 4-5: Purl 2 rnds.
RND 6-8: Knit 3 rnds.
RND 9: (K2tog, K7, K2tog) twice. (18 sts)
RND 10-12: Knit 3 rnds.
RND 13: (K2tog, K5, K2tog) twice. (14 sts)
RND 14-16: Knit 3 rnds.

Continue to work decrease rounds, adding stuffing as you go.

RND 17: (K2tog, K3, K2tog) twice. (10 sts)
RND 18-19: Knit 2 rnds.
RND 25: (K2tog, K1, K2tog) twice. (6 sts)

Cut yarn and thread through remaining 6 sts (adding more stuffing if required). Pull to tighten and se-cure, leaving a small hole for sewing the head to the body.

Weave in ends.

HOOD
Using sand yarn (color 31) make a closed magic ring of 6 sts.

Distribute sts across 3 DPNs, place marker and begin working in rounds.

RND 1: Kfb 6 times. (12 sts)
RND 2: (Kfb, K1) 6 times. (18 sts)
RND 3: (Kfb, K2) 6 times. (24 sts)
RND 4: (Kfb, K3) 6 times. (30 sts)
RND 5: (Kfb, K4) 6 times. (36 sts)
RND 6: (Kfb, K5) 6 times. (42 sts)
RND 7: (Kfb, K6) 6 times. (48 sts)
RND 8: (Kfb, K7) 6 times. (54 sts)
RND 9-21: Knit 13 rnds.

Begin working flat.

Turn work to the wrong side.

Row 22: P2tog, P to last 2 sts, P2tog. (52 sts)
Row 23: K2tog, K to last 2 sts, K2tog. (50 sts)
Row 24: K2tog, K15, K2tog, K14, K2tog, K15. (47 sts)
Row 25: Knit.
Row 26: K2tog, K14, K2tog, K13, K2tog, K14. (44 sts)
Row 27: K13, K2tog, K14, K2tog, K13. (42 sts)

Bind off.

ARMS (make 2)
Using sand yarn (color 31) CO 4 sts.

Knit as i-cord.

RND 1-10: Knit 10 rnds.

Do not stuff.

Cut yarn and thread through re-maining 4 sts, pull to tighten and secure.

Weave in ends.

TAIL
Using sand yarn (color 31) CO 7 sts.

Distribute sts across 3 DPNs, place marker and join for working in the round, being careful not to twist cast on edge.

RND 1-4: Knit 4 rnds.
RND 5: K2tog, K5. (6 sts)
RND 6-7: Knit 2 rnds.

Change brown yarn (color 111).
RND 8-9: Knit 2 rnds.
RND 10: K2tog 3 times. (3 sts)

Add stuffing.

Cut yarn and thread through re-maining 3 sts, pull to tighten and secure.

Weave in ends.

EARS

EAR 1
Using brown yarn (color 111) CO 12 sts.

Distribute sts across 3 DPNs, place marker and join for working in the round, being careful not to twist cast on edge.

RND 1-5: Knit 5 rnds.
RND 6: (Kfb, K2) 4 times.(16 sts)
RND 7-9: Knit 3 rnds.
RND 10: (Kfb, K3) 4 times. (20 sts)
RND 11-17: 7 Rnds K all (20 sts)
RND 18: (Kfb, K4) 4 times. (24 sts)
RND 19-22: Knit 4 rnds.
RND 23: (Kfb, K5) 4 times. (28 sts)
RND 24-26: Knit 3 rnds.
RND 27: (Kfb, K6) 4 times. (32 sts)
RND 28-30: Knit 3 rnds.
RND 31: (Kfb, K7) 4 times. (36 sts)
RND 32-36: Knit 5 rnds.

Change color to sendy. Color 31.
RND 37-38: Knit 2 rnds.
RND 39: (K2tog, K4) 6 times. (30 sts)
RND 40: Knit.
RND 41: (K2tog, K3) 6 times. (24 sts)
RND 42: (K2tog, K2) 6 times. (18 sts)
RND 43: (K2tog, K1) 6 times. (12 sts)
RND 44: K2tog 6 times. (6 sts)

Do not stuff.

Cut yarn and thread through re-maining 6 sts, pull to tighten and secure.

Weave in ends.

EAR 2
Knit as for Ear 1 but using brown yarn (color 111) only.

ASSEMBLING AND FINISHING

1. Knit all the parts.

2. Sew the head onto the body.

3. Sew the arms to the body.

4. Embroider the dolls hair using navy yarn (color 71).

5. Position the hood on the head and sew in place along the neck line.

6. Cut small circle fo brown felt and glue into place for left eye.

7. Sew on buttons for eyes.

8. Pin the ears in place then sew them to the hood.

9. Apply pink blush to cheeks.

10. Sew the tail to the body.